WHAT K-DRAMA DOES WRITE

REBECCA WYNICK

978-1-953074-21-8 paperback Rebecca Wynick

Book cover design by Rebecca Wynick and Canva

For Morgan~

who warned me that watching five K-dramas was the threshold for addiction. You were right.

Your creativity, humor, and curiosity inspire me.

CONTENTS

A NOTE ON NAMES

Side note on the referenced K-dramas: The spellings of the names of characters are sometimes unclear. What is in the subtitles (in translation) does not always match the streaming sites, IMBD, or other review sites when consulted for accuracy in the writing of this book. For example, sometimes Jun is noted as Joon. I have done my best to get the most accurate character spellings, but errors may be noted by native speakers of Korean. If you find any such error, please feel free to email me, and I will update the next printing of this book.

INTRODUCTION

What This Book Is and Isn't

This book isn't meant to teach you to write. Rather, it is a celebration and an appreciation of what Korean Drama does well. K-drama is so successful at building impactive storytelling that audiences are growing at an exponential rate. Who wouldn't want to cash in on that? I know many writers, and not a one doesn't want to build an audience. So how do they do that? This is the focus of this book.

K-drama writers know how to touch the heart of the viewer, so much so that they come back for more. Some viewers are so inspired that they even start taking Korean language lessons! Meanwhile, people from all different backgrounds around the world are binge-watching, even with the language barrier. That's more than just good acting— that's good storytelling. I , for one, wanted to learn the secrets to their success. First off, I don't speak Korean. So, yes, that means that I'm reading the Korean Dramas as I watch. I choose to watch un-dubbed so that I can see and hear the inflection in the emotions of the actors in real time and in a more believable format. The natural question is why? If I wanted to read, I could've just picked up a book. I do, dozens in a year. So why put the effort into what essentially is an Asian serial, a soap opera if you will? First off, I would counter that to label what K-drama is as a soap opera is to underestimate the skill in the writing, directing, filming, and acting skills encompassed by the art form. I would counter that a "limited series" label would be more accurate, but that is a moot point as the question remains the same. Time is in limited quantity, so why would a full-time college instructor and part-time novelist spend her few free hours in watching a drama and reading in translation?

However, before I spend the next hundred or so pages answering that question, I would like to flip the inquiry. How has anyone not watched the biggest growing genre on television? Likewise, if an aspiring writer, you have an obligation to view and read the trends to not only learn from others' successes but to take into account the emerging market and how to optimize that in your writing life. K-dramas are successful stories that people are clamoring for with a voracious appetite. According to numerous news outlets and articles on the subject, K-drama's growing segment of the entertainment market is taking the United States by storm— again by non-speakers of the language. Why? What makes it work? What is it in their storytelling that transcends language and cultural boundaries?

Some might say my attempt at analyzing is flawed; K-drama cannot teach writing skills or strategies. Only books and stories can teach people how to write books and stories. But I would contend that scripts are a precise and complicated level of writing on whose success relies upon realistic emotion and believability, especially when working in the fantasy genre, my chosen focus. Therefore, to aspire to have a dedicated and devoted following, the juggernaut that is the Korean Wave should not be ignored. The phenom of K-drama's exponential growth and ever widening world interest is worth analysis, not just as a media form, but as a possibility to tighten our own writing and perhaps expand our audience base. While K-drama is unique in its cultural context, the stylistic and story choices made by these writers can be broken into components that can be emulated.

K-drama is driving a market of television and expanding daily. If I could invest in it by buying stocks in K-Drama, I would. Some studios, such as Studio Dragon, are producing such a polished product that they have garnered a devoted fan-base, myself included. Plus, take into account that what we are seeing in the United States, while in translation, still resonates, and frankly, that's just good writing.

Chapter One

MAKING EVERY WORD COUNT

I find it interesting that some of the most powerful moments in Korean Drama don't have any words. So what does that mean for the writer? Setting, mood, and tone need to be created in the exposition so that the reader/viewer is immersed in the scene, and therefore, the story. Likewise, the characters' movements, expressions, and actions all have to be orchestrated. It means detailing your stories into seconds, and fractions of seconds. A flash of an eye in anger, a shaky hand, a hesitant pause before an impulsive act, those phrases we use to present a moment in real life. K-drama includes these emotions and actions so well. It could be those tiny moments are what is missing in your writing. Those nuanced instances that evoke so much connection in the viewer need to be first translated onto paper.

A visual analogy for this is how a cake is built. I doubt there is anyone you know that hasn't seen a master chef, or not-so-master amateur, construct a cake. We watch with rapt attention as the baker adds flavorings, both common and surprising, custards and fruit fillings, until ultimately ending in a sugary frosting and possibly questionable decor. The Korean Drama is built this way as well, one layer at a time.

It is clear from the onset that the K-drama has a developed

and multi-layered base structure to any chosen tale. Likewise, many writers have at least a base structure plotted before they write. (Plotters more so while Pantsers have more of a "suggestion" with some key points.) On this frame, the K-drama writers add each ingredient, (plot point, emotion, twist etc.) to their tale with a visible language. We will, for the time being, put set dressing aside, simply because it is a given that as a visual medium detail and attention has been made. The smallest of moments that define a character, emotions, and personal values have been attended to with great purpose and detail. It is almost as if the writers took a video of all human behavior and reduced the film to image-by-image in the replay. Every movement, facial tick, muscle clench, nervous gesture has been categorized, defined, and employed— first by stage direction and then in action. Even an eyelash flick, a soft groan, or a slow movement has been scripted. Each movement, each word counts.

The question you have to ask is, if your text isn't adding, yes, even one line at a time, then why is it there?

What viewers sometimes forget or fail to notice is that K-drama in its compact form, is rich with dimensional layers, but limited in space and time for dialogue. A whole world must be presented at the onset of the opening scene with the subsequent pace never lagging. Therefore, dialogue is vastly important. Likewise, dialogue cannot compensate for a poorly thought out or fleshed out plot. Perhaps this is its strength.

By nature, Korean Drama is forced to show not tell— a phrase overly used and frustrating when used as advice to new writers. That is not to say that it isn't accurate. However, the gestures, movements, and mood are written into the script, with the same directions. One must "show" the story, make the emotions clear, reveal the suffering or the stress of the situation, and most importantly, take us along. In K-drama, as in life, sometimes one look says it all. So your job, as the writer, is to evoke that image and meaning. That emotionality earns you loyal fans of the K-drama format. They crave and enjoy the sentimentality, emotion, and that connection that occurs on the molecular level, one word at a time.

Show, Don't Tell

Often common writing advice is show, don't tell. Then the follow up question is, how? In "show, don't tell", actors have an advantage because K-dramas are a visual medium. However, we as writers can take notes from what they are doing. How better to show but with a show. Let me explain... If an actor wipes away a tear or perhaps replaces visible despair with a forced smile, how did that actor know to do that? With words, a script, stage directions— writing. Through analyzing the draw and fervor of Korean drama, I found many ways to improve my own writing.

Maybe I am a slow learner. I'd heard the words many times, "Show, don't tell". Sometimes words are the tipping point, and instead, visual cues are needed. But for the life of me, as I looked at my new words scattered across the page, I thought I had done just that. What did my Beta readers mean? What was my editor advising me to do? I could repeat their advice almost verbatim. I could see their comments in the margins of my document. The truth was that I was too close to the work to be objective any more. I even fell back on the excuse, "They just don't understand what I am trying to do here", which, in all honesty, is a cop out. That kind of mentality is a way to assuage the ego and perhaps bolster my own feelings of worth and intelligence. And I was wrong. Every. Single. Time.

If you are lucky enough to have a writing group like mine, Alpha and Beta readers, and a professional editor or two, listen to them. If they say "show", they mean it. Argue all you want to yourself and then step back and look, really look at what you have produced. If you dropped dead tomorrow, would they be able to see your vision for your characters and your story from the words alone? I thought so, but then they corrected me of my delusions. So what was I doing wrong? Writing isn't like a math class where you find the errant integer and then all is solved. There are so many layers of issues, plot lines, complex characters, and the like. There is no simple solution— except "show, don't tell".

Much like Abbott and Costello and "Who's on First" routine, I was confused beyond redemption until I landed on a Korean Drama series. Me, the woman who spends her days teaching writing and literary analysis was sucked into the phenom of the pop serial. And it clutched me by the heart within the first five minutes (which equates to the author's first page.) They'd done it. Hooked me at the start, had me caring for the characters as if they were my own family, best friend, or colleague. I cried and laughed with them and was deeply invested in their lives, mesmerized by a language I don't speak from a culture to which I had no connection.

So the question was how? How did they do it? Five Korean drama series later (the number my offspring swore was the "addiction threshold", I wanted more and scanned the tv listings for the next target of my emotional obsession. Again, this is from someone who adores and Mastered in 18th and 19th century literature, who reads *Wuthering Heights* almost yearly, and will concede that Austen fans are not wrong in their devotion. What Austen does in pages and pages of narration and introspection Korean Drama reveals in seconds or minutes with as much poignancy, stakes, and emotion. That's when I realized the solution to my problem. K-drama's very medium was the key to my lack of understanding. They were showing. Especially to viewers like me that had to watch in translation. We all know that no translation is perfect, and oftentimes, I mentally re-translated what should've been said based on what I was viewing. To fully understand the emotional and sometimes physical stakes, I had to watch carefully for facial ticks, nervous hand gestures, posturing, and tone. How something is said is as important as what is said. They were showing me their meaning in every movement and pause, each glance and avoidance cue. Showing.

Now I understood. K-drama's world-wide appeal transcended language barriers because of its clarity of vision. I could see meaning even if I disagreed with the word choice in the subtitles. Their purpose was clear. I felt the intent. Now I, the writer, had to attempt to create the vision I saw for my own characters as clearly for my own readers. I had to put into words specifically what I see when my characters live in my mind. And I used the tricks and strategies K-drama taught me to make that happen.

If you don't yet watch Korean dramas, I suggest you do. If you already are a fan, I hope this makes you appreciate the genius behind the direction and script work. Most of the dramas I watched were predominately on Netflix, not a bias on my part, just what I had access to for viewing.

Because This Is My First Life was my gateway K-drama. One season and I was hooked, line, sinker, and sunk. Never before had I been invested in characters, so quickly, nor so deeply. As a writer, I asked myself why.

These ultimately were the lessons I initially learned from *Because This Is My First Life,* and this book attempts to share and illustrate these for you with assorted K-drama favorites.

Lessons learned:

- slow down with details
- flesh out ticks
- find your characters' strengths, biases, and breaking points
- identify what makes your protagonist / antagonist uniquely them
- Reveal these character traits in snippets (no one wants an info dump)

- Explore more by engaging your main characters with others. It's in those connections and situations that reveal info in an organic manner. Your characters might even surprise you. Place them in a situation and see what they do.
- True love evolves slowly
- A believable character is best shown in daily habits, challenges, and small choices
- All action yields a reaction, and in that reaction, sometimes there is a revelation

While I am not claiming to have learned how to apply this successfully (yet) to my own writing, I can at least identify the components employed. It is my hope that this book helps you to reflect on your writing and perhaps enhance or encourage your viewership of the K-drama wave that is taking over the world.

As a note, reader and viewer in this book can be used almost interchangeably because as an author, isn't the goal the same? We all want engaging characters that people connect with to create brand loyalty and invest in you, the creator. All of the included references to specific K-dramas, except one, could be classified as "highly recommend". I am in awe of the range and depth of these actors and the studios that produce them.

Small Moments

Small events can have a big pay off. Every day doesn't have to have a huge battle involving the rescue of a small child or a cliffhanger. These are not the moments that keep the viewer or reader turning pages or tuning in to the show. Some of the current box office movies rely upon the flash, the bang, and the amazement. But these are not the stories that linger. After the initial oohs and ahhs, the conversation will turn to other things of substance. Most will not return even for a re-watch. They've seen what the film has to offer, and there is no lingering discussion or pondering thoughts (unless of course there is a plot hole to be debated). However, substance lingers on the mind like the taste of a fine wine, its memory recalled to analyze and muse over. The moment is savored and a part of us; whether we know it or not, we have been enlarged from the experience. "Enriched" would have been an obvious word choice here, but in this case I mean enlarged. We, the writers, are enlarging the scope and scale of the human experience, our boundaries of what is the norm, and those possibilities widen our fan base and reach.

In small moments we reveal our humanity, and this can have a huge pay-off on emotion. For example, a mother returns a candy at the check out to the disappointment of the child and then exchanges it for the cheaper banana to satisfy the child's sweet tooth. The reality is the mother does not eat, the banana costing her her own meal. We've seen a version of this played out before, but it is in the small things that richness can be derived (much like modern flower arranging).

We have opportunity to reveal in these small actions secret truths. These create two results: the reader at the edge of his or her seat, and reveals much of the value system of the characters.

It All Begins with a Gesture

In *My Unfamiliar Family*, the drama portrays a family who lives as strangers. Disengaged for assorted reasoning, it is a study of gestures. Following the father's decent into dementia, we see eyes shift and change with emotion; they widen, curve upwards at the side showing hope. The jumpy leg twitch tells us when the characters are lying. Use the visual cues the actors are providing the audiences. For example, imagine a loving father's eyes versus cold eyes. Same face, but what changed to show you this? Maybe spend some time in the mirror trying to see what it was the actor did and then write that. If it's a matter of cultural nuances, describe within limits and not with a huge backstory dump. Maybe add a modifier to indicate that the hand gesture was dismissive but nothing more. Let the readers add their perception of how that looks and feels, much like viewers add their own experiences with love and loss to create the syntax within themselves and the actors.

As humans we naturally take cues in an instant. This is a carryover from the hunter / survival instinct. For example, you know at a glance if you can ask your parents for money or if it is a good time to ask your wife if she'd mind you taking a weekend off from the kids to go hang with your buddies. We measure those quick glances and proceed as they indicate, sometimes tiptoeing away. We need to take the time to impart that nuance to your reader. Provide quality in a few words, a pursed lip, a flush of color, an eye tick. Just don't overwrite it.

Perhaps the best way not to overwrite is to create a chart of ideas for certain emotions. Choose one or two for your character and don't explain it. For example here a few unnecessary wordings. What's in the parenthesis is not needed.

She looked away (in shame).

Shook head (no).

She blushed (shyly).

Your audience or readers are not idiots. Less is more. Let them bridge the gap. When they personalize it with their own emotion, then the characters become real, and isn't that what we want? Television, at least American television, tends to explain—a lot. And it is annoying. Trust your reader. Let them feel and anticipate. *Because This Is My First Life* was all about subtleties and nuance. Watch the drama and see if your can see the subscript in the actors' moves that had to be dictated by a great writer and director.

Just because you know every detail doesn't mean you should share it. Trust the reader / viewer to fill in the historical gaps. It is in that space that the work resonates because each reader can connect with the text and complete the writing.

An example of this is in the omission of sex in *Romance Is a Bonus Book*. When Eun-ho opens his shirt and asks why should he get pajamas after he'd already asked to sleep in Dan-i's room that night, she bashfully turns away and turns the light off. Did you really need to see more? Does the author need to literally spell out what they will be up to in that room and bed? What we do know is that he will be bold and playful while considerate to her just as we know that she will be awkward and nervous. Those traits were already built into these characters. We saw her straightening the pillows over and over again, a physical demonstration of her nerves. Those small actions defined them and the start of their sexual relationship better than a bunch on interior monologues or unneeded description. Does this mean we should write like a screenwriter? Maybe.

Visualize and then decide what words are really needed like you are buying the stage setting materials out of your own pocket. You will agree then that less is indeed more.

Underwrite

Underwrite, however, be careful. Just as you can overwrite a scene, you should find what point do you balance effective editing versus underwriting? Stephen King famously said, "Kill your darlings". He wasn't wrong. Don't insult your reader. You do not need to explain every detail nor describe in depth the color of a character's eyes. In Korean Drama a movement or a glance often takes the place of words. It's the nuance of the mood that captures our interest, not the tedious backstory, unending narration, and didactic morality.

It is in the gap between the words and the action that the readers or viewers form their own thoughts and engage in the story. If you have painstakingly identified every emotion and reaction, your audience has nothing to contribute to the work. You want your audience hooked, and that means they have to invest. They have to find a connection, meaning, and have the space to wonder and extend the piece beyond the page and the screen.

This may seem counter-intuitive. You may ask, shouldn't I present a fully-fleshed world? Yes, but. The but is do not get so far into the minutia that you are telling instead of showing. Do not proselytize but lead. Trust your audience to draw conclusions. So what if each reader sees a slightly different variant of what you created in your head? Personal interpretation can and should enrich the experience. You want the audience to connect, like synapses in the brain. Show me nervousness in a gesture, not by having the character say he or she is nervous, or worse yet, having another character act as a narrator and declare, "You look nervous". That kind of insulting dialogue will have me dropping the book or drama faster than a hot coal.

BECAUSE THIS IS MY FIRST LIFE (2017)

Writer: Yoon Nan-joong
Genre: Rom-Com
Produced by: Studio Dragon

The premise begins when See Hee, a fastidious and socially awkward computer software designer, accidentally rents out a room in his home to a female. Likewise, the tenant, Ji-Ho, believes she is renting from a female. Several days pass without either of them crossing paths, comically, with near misses due to their opposing work schedules. This seems to suit them just fine since the rental agreement was about finances, not forging a friendship. Upon finally meeting, the situation causes social and moral problems. However, their living habits seem to be thus far compatible, so they agree to a "socially acceptable" marriage in order to continue with their living arrangement, even going so far as to sign a contract. Eventually their common values, behaviors, compatible personalities, and similar temperaments lead to love. A charming story filled with moments of comedic timing, *Because This Is My First Life's* plot is rounded out with an ensemble cast with their own engaging secondary plot lines.

ROMANCE IS A BONUS BOOK (2019)

Writer: Jung Hyun-jung
Genre: Romance with comedic elements
Produced by: Studio Dragon

The drama follows Kang Dan-i as she attempts to rebuild her life after a divorce. Years out of the employment market due to sacrificing her professional goals for her marital and parental responsibilities has left Dan-i in the uncomfortable spot of being too old for an entry level position but too inexperienced for anything better. Now homeless and destitute, she resourcefully relies on her old friend, Eun-ho, unbeknownst to him, by working as his cleaning woman and secret boarder.

Eun-ho's star has risen as he is both a renowned writer and an editor-in-chief. When Dan-i acquires an internship at his publishing house, Eun-ho does what he can to support Dan-i as she struggles to fit in at work while suppressing the love he's long held for her.

This drama effectively portrays the challenges women face when attempting to return to the workforce after a stint as homemaker with the agist responses of younger colleagues and the biting disdain of life-long career women.

Dan-i's life choices make her appear significantly older than the handful of years between herself and Eun-ho, making this attraction to her life-long friend feel like a December - May romance. A complicated yet sweet romance ensues when these biases are removed.

Chapter Two

CHARACTER DEVELOPMENT

I think the thing K-drama does best is create characters we believe are human— especially those that are not. Their humanity makes us invest in their storylines, root for the doomed hero, and cry with the cast when a beloved character feels joy, pain, or passes into the next world. How they do this is the question.

Each and everyone of us has a quirk, behavior, gesture, or obsession (for lack of a better word), that our loved ones learn to tolerate or perhaps our friends mock us for. This behavior can be irrational or merely endearing, but it is a clear declaration of humanity. It is the "tell" that reveals ourselves to those who know us best.

The challenge for the writers is that we really need to get to know our characters for a quirk to be believable. A trait cannot simply be assigned, like a plot point. It must be based on a belief, fear, habit, or familial mannerisms. Quirks are key to knowing more about our main characters, to endear or repulse. Its careful and purposeful construction helps us buy in, and therefore, tune in episode after episode. It is because of this we no longer see actors on a screen but rather real people— our friends. And that relationship is priceless.

The believability of the characters is the key to the audience caring and engagement. We invest in people stories. Readers cannot and will not relate to characters that are too perfect, not even the hero. (Think Han Solo, all the more delicious for his flaws.) We may admire them, be jealous of them, or lust after them— but relate? Not going to happen without a clear connection. Korean Drama fixes that in that they present characters that are flawed in a realistic and sometimes endearing way.

Main characters or pivotal side characters should have a problem that the audience can relate to in some way. Likewise, the studios are not afraid to let their hero or heroine address topics and issues that may be deemed taboo. Perhaps it is because of this handling of the main characters that K-drama has an intensely dedicated audience, and its reach is spreading across the globe. After all, universal issues foster a global community and transcends all language barriers. A marvelous side effect of this deeply vested writing is greater cultural understanding and empathy. This is important to note, especially if your work is meant to evoke change in social norms.

A prime example of taking on social issues that were normally hidden behind closed doors in a drama is *It's Okay Not to Be Okay.* The drama shows us broken families, childhood traumas, mental illness, abandonment issues, fear of connection, familial obligation, and betrayals. The small circle of friends also serves to reveal how characters develop and maintain relationships as well as how the characters are perceived and interact with the others. These character traits and interactions illuminate what would've otherwise required pages of backstory or narrative. The side characters act as a mirror to the main characters' true selves. That self is usually only learned through time and experience. Honestly, readers and viewers don't want to wade through pages and pages of narrative. The circle of friends, those that the main characters interact with gives you, the viewer, assorted angles of characterization simultaneously in that each secondary character knows the main character based on his or her interactions or "truths". Likewise, a best friend versus a girlfriend or a parent would interpret the character's actions based on his or her knowledge of the issue at hand. These interpretations could appear to be contradictory, but taken together, will reveal more in a moment than even the main character would acknowledge.

Ironically, characters don't always know themselves when faced with a dilemma. So faced with a problem, surrounded by friends or family with varied point of view, is valuable to reveal even hidden sides of a psyche. Try placing your character in a situation and then interact with different people What do you learn? Just as you would tell your best friends a different story than say to a parent, what nugget of truth is revealed in the omission? Even a lie or a half truth digression is revealing. Likewise, how the situation is handled, who supports the character, and who challenges him or her, are all valuable conduits of characterization.

Onions

People don't live in a vacuum, nor should your characters. Otherwise, plot is a straight line with no suspense and no mystery. Likewise, these characters don't always understand their own motives, let alone others. Rather they reveal self and their psyche over time such as in *My Unfamiliar Family*, *Hotel del Luna*, and *Run On*. Think of the onion, a common metaphor. You should, much like peeling an onion, reveal background, story, and plot in micro layers.

Avoid the info dump, that long, narrative backstory that is common in some novels and that bores you to tears. When this happens there is no character to discover and fall in love with over time because the author has already given you a capsule summary that either is pleasing or not. Avoid, avoid, avoid the info dump. K-drama does this masterfully, revealing only bits of truth as it is needed or to surprise, and just when you thought you had him or her figured out. Humans are complicated characters that are adept at hiding, even from ourselves, who we really are. These dramas know this and capitalize on it. Think too, about that "get to know you" first date. If someone you just met told you everything, (And I mean *everything*), good or bad, in your first meeting, you wouldn't want more. You'd run. So why do this in your written work? (Ie: She is seventeen years old, blue eyes, her nose is bent from a missed softball, neglected by her father, she bites her lip to hide the teeth that have needed braces but that her family couldn't afford, and she hopes he won't see that she has three cavities with untrendy silver fillings. BLEH.)

Instead, we, the writers, should be like a toddler and ask "Why?", both often and frequently about our characters and as we write them. For example:

She's hungry so she steals.

Why? Why is she so hungry?

Maybe her parents kicked her out of the house.

Why?

Maybe she is pregnant and not allowed back at school.

What K-drama does masterfully is dig into these layers, the writers asking the right questions, and revealing these layers only as needed.

Emotion

K-drama is elegant in the use of emotion, and it knows that emotion is the most effective and poignant hook. However, fight the urge to grab your reader immediately with a big scene; that's all flash and no substance. While viewers may enjoy the lark of a Marvel movie extravaganza in an opener, it is the substance that keeps them coming back for more K-dramas, week after week, ravenously seeking episode after episode, much like we want readers to turn our pages and reach for the next chapter. We must use a light hand with deep implications to keep the reader reading.

As infants our first instinct is to reach for human connection. So how does K-drama purposely seek to connect with audiences? A shared reality results in human connection. Now we are curious. Why is she moving? Why is that grandmother crying? Why did he punch the wall? Curious readers stay connected— for now. At least until we blow it. But for now they are willing to sit and watch or turn the page to find out more. So, now we need to deepen the connection by providing endearing and humanizing layers to our characters (twitches, ticks, mannerism, a crooked smile). We need to include clues but not all of what's at stake. Tantalize but do not slide into the info dump. For example, In *It's Okay Not to Be Okay* we learn that Gang-tae worries that they will have to move again. In those few words we realize this behavior of Sang-tae has caused problems before, in fact numerous times, and that his brother is exhausted from their constantly shifting landscape and having to establish himself once again. Pages of info about their family life was revealed in moments. Reveal in not just words but subtle actions the character's thoughts (sighing, nervousness, etc.) and then evolve to action so that we feel that we are watching the emotions roll over as they process the options.

Empathy and Flaws

With skilled emotional manipulation the final result is we become part of those families and characters' lives— or at least we wish we were. Their suffering makes us cry and their joys do, too. We cry when they cry. Our hearts are broken when we see their's break. We feel the chill of the cold rain and their despair because of the nuances created by the writers endear them to us and make us believe, at least for a short time, that what is on the screen really does matter. Their disappointments become ours.

It all circles back to the character development. Everything really does; it starts and ends there ultimately. We see their character flaws and love them because of them. They become real to us, and therefore, relatable. We empathize with the poor choices that they make, and their flawed judgements. It may actually be why we connect to him or her, especially if we can understand why they make the choices they do.

This also makes them fleshed out and three-dimensional. Good authors know their characters and don't utilize any of them as mere 2-D plot devices.

So how do you do this? You love your characters, and trust me, the reader wants to, too. That is why they picked up the book. They wanted to be moved. They want to engage with your story and be transported far away or to connect with a relatable emotion to perhaps help them navigate a harsh and demanding world. So how do we fulfill their hopes? We follow the K-drama lead.

Don't make your characters perfect. No one can live up to that, and no one, certainly, can relate to it either. Even in classic literature such as with Heathcliff and Mr. Darcy, we see their failings. Both gentlemen, bastards in their own right, they most certainly are flawed, broken men, and we love them for it.

It is tempting to write our hero or love interest as the epitome of ___________ (author fills in blank here.) Because why else would we be interested in said character, we mutter to ourselves. Don't we want someone we can emulate or admire? Or perhaps even lust after (said every romance novel ever). But it is in the flaws that make these characters real, three-dimensional, and we love them all the more for it.

The bottom line is, no matter how attractive, witty, or talented a character may seem, it is his or her humanity that we ultimately connect with, and that connection builds reader loyalty and devotion. Perfection is boring. It is in the nuances that our characters come alive. No one wants to be best friends with perfection. And we certainly don't want to date it. Book "crushes" and pining occurs all the time, and it's never with the infallible.

Bottom line is we want believable characters, even in fantasy, so that we can make connections with their humanity. We want to feel and experience life with our characters. And as readers, and viewers, we want to care. That desire sometimes carries over to life-long impact as we learn the lessons they learn and become wary when faced with certain scenarios explored in these dramas. This empathy crosses all genres.

Empathy usually starts with a common situation that most, if not all, can recognize, a shared situation that the readers or viewers can then tie in their own life experiences and recall that feeling of pain, frustration, despair, or helplessness and therefore multiply the impact of the scene. For example, in *It's Okay Not to Be Okay*, the common situation is of supervising a sibling or family member and that familial obligation causes problems with a job. The reader or viewer can convert their frustrations of babysitting a family member or the stress of providing care for a dependent into the scene with the brothers, thus creating a shared experience.

Conflict

Conflict needs to be relatable, realistic, and with stakes. You need the audience to care about the outcome. Be sure to make the trauma look personal. Do not paint with broad strokes or vague generalities. Take the reader along with emotional details.

Then add the fine details. Everyone suffers differently, but it is in the differences that we find the individual. If we believe in the trauma, then we emote as readers. To make this work, you need to know your characters. Build an emotion chart. (Just a basic chart with three columns: character name, situation, character's action.Repeat, repeat, repeat.) Test them in varied situations and gauge their responses. Some of you may be saying, "I don't know what (character name) would do during a house fire. Well, that's the point. Start small. What would your character run to save first? Build from there. That's why charting works. Each answer helps build the next. None of your characters will be believable if their reactions and emotions don't match the character you have been building, and your readers will disengage as a result.

Yes, you want to lure your readers in, but once you have them hooked, you have to keep them on the line. I am sure I am not the only one who was invested in a story and something reads false. Maybe it was poor editing, our maybe the character you were expecting took an unexpected turn. But if the character shifts in a way that he or she is not longer believable, the magic is removed, and the reader is sitting stunned, as if a bucket of cold water was doused over his or her head. I hate when I am invested in a character's story and then betrayed. I personally read (and write) to escape, so to be plummeted to earth on an ill thought out idea sucks the magical illusion away. It feels like a betrayal, or poor planning, and I will never read that author's words again.

Readers need a well-thought out personal narrative with a very clearly defined backstory, whether we reveal that to the reader or not. We, the writers, need to know our characters. So take them on "what if" journeys and chart their responses. You'll learn a lot about their character and therefore, be ready to build on their personality for your reader.

One idea that could work to imitate what K-drama seems to do effortlessly is to create an emotion chart. You would do this to practice how you can show emotion while making sure that the reactions are character-specific.

The chart could have an emotion / next column character name / and his or her way of showing this.

For example: emotion: nervousness / Who: Har-i / Actions: cleaning, ducking shoulders, hides face etc.

Doubt and Inner Conflict

Doubt is a powerful emotion that causes mayhem. Most often when we write characters' stories, we move them purposely through our plot. However, if we employ doubt, it's largely through internal exposition. Doubt in K-drama has significantly more impact. Sometimes whole series can turn on doubt or a misunderstanding. It is actionable, dictating movement, choice, or the crippling conundrum in the lack of decision.

Inner conflict is revealed slowly, because if we truly understood our own emotions, would we have any problems? K-dramas know this and reveal these doubts and conflicts (and subsequent avoidance of the same) much like a person would in real life. There is clearly a plan to the backstory, but the surprises and discovery are the ones shared by the protagonist. This creates twists or new truths as more of the inner puzzle or turmoil of a person's psychic unravelling.

Doubts can create angst and turmoil. Insecurities aren't scripted in stories or done as well as the K-dramas. Sure, we might show our character's flaws, but doubt is more elusive and situational, revealing itself as needed and not before. If doubt was upfront, it could be dealt with (or belittled). The drama handing is more organic, and therefore, desirable to the audience.

Dialogue

Dialogue is invaluable in characterization. The word choice not only indicates the education level of a person but social standing. A dialect can also be assumed by a character, indicating a rejection of the status to which he or she was born. Even lack of speech can be revealing. Add to this the interactions with others and how the dialogue of the main character changes to suit each situation or relationship, and nuances of the character is revealed. Does the character speak with respect to an elder or with impatience and disdain? Is the loved one honored or merely tolerated? Is he or she abrupt with those who work in subservient positions or to those who are socially marginalized? It has been commonly stated that how we treat those from whom we have nothing to gain indicates our true values and beliefs.

Dialogue is where word choice is particularly important. Everyone knows that people aren't as honest as they could be, and a fictional character is no different. Likewise, what a character does may contradict what is said. What is said could gloss over the pain that is felt. The question is why? What is he or she hiding and from whom? So word choice, especially in emotional scenes where the character may need to let down his or her guard, may be frustrated, heart-broken, and filled with anger, or may reveal a carefully orchestrated facade. Through dialogue, chinks in the carefully coiffed personal armor may appear or walls could be built, thus causing more conflict. Meanwhile the shifts in language, or an inconsistency, may lead the audience to confusion or a mystery. That is why the most reliable use of dialogue is with accompanying physical movement. It is best to have the characters' emotions play out with an associated physical tick, a clenched jaw, or a shudder, and then your character becomes more dimensional and believable. The more we believe, the more we connect.

Ultimately, while a reader may be seeking an escape, to the

characters , however, they want a connection so that the fiction touches their hearts.

The Anti-Hero

The anti-hero, even if the intention is to make him or her a leading character, is often not likable. However, to neglect this character and subsequent development is a mistake that will yield a two-dimensional character. The bad guy will become nothing more than a character in a poorly developed action film or comic book movie. Marvel knows that the bad guy is a hero in his or her own mind, and has worked to develop the anti-hero to the benefit of movie sales. The antagonist cannot only be rationalized by a rich backstory. Prior events shaped the characters into what he or she has become. Our job as writers is to flesh this out.

In *Doona!* (2023), the main character by the same name is not likable. Immature, cruel, taunting in the first few episodes. I struggled to keep watching. But slowly, this antagonist became a compelling character with numerous justifications for her behaviors.

The Supernatural

Even in fantasy, like in *Hotel del Luna* or *The Uncanny Counter* or any of the K-dramas where a character is a ghost, the fantastical characters have very realistic limitations and human failings. This makes the character not only more believable but relatable.

They can hold a grudge — and boy, do they.

They are not impervious to physical and and emotional pain

or injuries unlike older superhero movies that remained two-dimensional and relied upon the action scenes.

Characteristics that can be developed are: internal strengths and advantages, hang ups, childhood trauma, physical and emotional scars, shown by memories (or hauntings) or evidence of emotional baggage.

HOTEL DEL LUNA (2019)

Writers: Hong Jung-sun and Hong Mi-ran
Genre: Dark Fantasy, Romance, ensemble cast
Produced by: Studio Dragon

Hotel del Luna's clientele are souls readying to cross over into the afterlife. Man-wol, the hotel caretaker, is soul bound, and has been for centuries, to serve those newly deceased. She provides for their needs so that they can complete unfinished business and release grudges in this life and cross over to what lies beyond. At the center of the hotel is a enchanted guardian tree that flourishes or wilts based on the actions and choices of the current caretaker. Unfortunately, Man-wol's heart has hardened into a selfish, frivolous, and greedy overseer. In contrast, the hotel is staffed by a collection of endearing characters with their own unfinished business and long-held grudges. Their stories, over numerous centuries, are eventually revealed, and their reasoning for lingering on the human plain is resolved. However, Man-wol, bound by a deity to ages of service, was meant to use this opportunity to learn and grown as she served her penance. Her reluctance to do so means Man-wol's time on earth may be up soon. She has to learn to love and forgive or face a fate worse than the one she has been living.

Fantastical and sometimes gory events in varied historical settings make this an engaging and emotional tale, rich in character development, motivation, and numerous plot lines. *Hotel Del Luna* combines mythology and fantasy into a storyline that is both memorable for its innovation and character development. These characters are flawed and endearing, while believable in what should be an unbelievable setting. It is a skilled balancing act that these writers achieve. Cultural myths are represented in an accessible manner for those not previously knowledgeable. The fantastical components have rules.

This drama is a good one for analyzing how magical worlds and fantasy must have an underlying structure, and it is in the groundwork that the subsequent story is built. The rules create a framework for the characters' interactions and limitations. The main characters, and there are several, in this drama all have an emotional depth which is a momentous undertaking. Likewise, each side character has a fully fleshed out backstory of his or her own.

IT'S OKAY NOT TO BE OKAY (2020)

(Literal translation: *Psycho, but It's Okay*)

Writer: Jo long
Genre: fantasy, drama, trauma-induced mental illness drama
Produced by: Studio Dragon

With a quick nod to the movie *Rain Man* in the opening scene, *It's Okay to Not Be Okay* opens with two brothers, Moon Gang-tae, a hospital orderly, who cares for his older, autistic brother, Sang-tae. Gang-tae is forced to change jobs and move often due to his brother's continued struggles with dramatic, emotional outbursts. Frequently triggered, Sang-tae has been scarred due to witnessing their mother's murder. Gang-tae sacrifices his own stability, education, and employment opportunities to keep their small family intact and protect his brother from being housed in a care facility. It is clear the loving relationship between the brothers is the key to their survival.

However, when Gang-tae and Sang-tae cross paths with the antisocial children's book writer, Moon-young, their lives get complicated and filled with surprise. Sang-tae had long been a fan of Ms. Ko's books, committing them to memory with his obsessive re-reading, so he is thrilled to meet the troubled writer who is fighting demons of her own. The children's book writer in this tale, Moon-young is not easily classified. She is clearly traumatized and struggles with mental illness, but this drama does not make a caricature of her nor the irony that she writes beloved children's stories. Over time we learn that all three of the main characters deal with trauma and the sub-sequential scars that those horrors cause. This drama excels with illustrating how well people hide trauma.

This K-drama is often labelled as a Rom-Com. I disagree; there is far too much drama for comedy, and the romance is negligible. It is a seeming pairing of opposites with Gang-tae's gentle and compassionate mannerisms and Moon-young's often vile and bitter social interactions. But together they eventually find healing and comfort. The main characters of *It's Okay Not to Be Okay* lives intertwine, providing opportunity for both healing of unspoken traumas and codependency. Both dark and humorous at times, it's a tale that tugs at the heart so much so that you root for each of the main characters growth and wish for their ability to overcome their own personal ghosts.

It's Okay Not to Be Okay is a great example of handling mental illness without stereotypes. It represents autism without the character becoming the hero or an overly sugar-coated "cute" character with a guaranteed happy ending. Realism in the depiction of the challenges of daily life makes this drama powerful and moving. Sang-tae's character is deeper and more multifaceted as a result. None of the key protagonists is a hero, but there's a balanced representation of all the characters involved.

OUR UNWRITTEN SEOUL (2025)

Writer Lee Kang
Genre: family drama
Produced by: Monster / Studio Dragon

The story is of two sisters, twins Mi-Rae (meaning future) and Mi-ji (meaning unknown). Identical twins formed and limited by illness, education, physical talent, and familial expectation. Both girls are constantly pitted against the other as if their two distinct paths had been foretold in the stars. However, tragically their own mother can't tell them apart. She constantly confuses one with the other, a situation they take advantage of on several occasions.

Family pressure creates feelings of inadequacy and insecurity. It also hastens the urgency of their search for identity since so many try to limit them and define them, regardless of their personal objections or feelings. These young women are socially measured and actively feel crippling self-doubt. The restrictions of meeting others' expectations and limits in the name of reason and love wall them in, and each much find a way to the find who she truly is meant to be.

Chapter Three

SIDE CHARACTERS

Are there really "side" characters in life? A "side of characters" yields a more fleshed out world. They are key to avoiding info dumps for backstory. As the main character interacts with others, he or she is likewise revealed by those interactions. So much is revealed by how he or she treats others. What K-drama gets fantastically right are nuanced behavior, ticks, twitches, and tells.

The main character's friends and acquaintances are useful for revealing secrets from the past— usually at the most inopportune time. Loyalties are revealed. Sometimes these characters from the past explain the quirky reasoning behind the actions the main character takes. Sometimes childhood friends reveal long-hidden or avoided family issues. But since they are on the "inside" of the main character's history, they are the key to solving deceptive and confusing behavior.

These characters can sometimes explain how their friendship serves as chosen family and why. Do your Beta readers say your main character lacks depth? Add a history or a past life. Be careful when you link between the present day friend and the past. Do so in an organic manner rather than forced exposition for the sake of clarifying why the main character is behaving as he is.

One thing that could be explored is does the main character grow with or outgrow these other relationships? A friend from the past might be just that, old news. Maybe your protagonist has evolved from his or her origin. These side characters are also reminders of past promises, bad decisions, early love, and values. Whether that has changed or not can be reflected by facing these moments of the past. Characters from the past can also say or show what others cannot, such as the secrets of prior behaviors. (*Hotel del Luna* is a prime example). Does the main character (MC) turn away from past obligations or is his or her reasoning dangerously set in the past and not evolving to serve either his or her own needs or what makes sense now?

More character development can happen in these interactions with others, including sometimes uncomfortable moments. These reminders of the past promises brings out not only who the character was but who he or she is now. What is valued now? What will be risked? What has changed? What remains the same? Which promises will be honored? Is the MC a person of his or her word or does the MC shift as time passes? Does an increase in personal wealth make the main character deny his or her own past or companions? Or does the main character embrace the roots that formed his or her character? There are both good and bad traits that can be explored here. If the MC clings to the past despite others moving on, it could reveal that he or she is stubborn and short-sighted. Does the MC reject past duty and debt? If so, is this MC fickle or wise? Whether you use it directly in your writing or not, explore the link between now and the past. See how it helps you build depth in your character's backstory, remembering that all you know isn't necessarily what your readers need to know, at least not in full.

Side characters are often the keepers of a living diary of accounts. Who truly is your main character? In fact, it is often difficult to build characters, because how can you know a character until you build him or her? Throw in others and see how they react. Add a secret. Does the character own it or run, or worse yet, lie and deny? Side characters are ripe opportunities for primary character development.

A friend's memories can last long. Think about all those stories old friends tell when they reunite around a dinner table. What bad decision or foibles do they reveal? And did we grow from those moments?

However, there is a big difference between neighborhood side characters, work colleagues, and friends both old and new. The new neighborhood reveals who the character is in a community setting (ie: *Hometown Cha Cha Cha*, *Dear My Friends*, *Crash Landing on You*). It defines the main character's sense of obligation to others and sense of civic duty.

An important thing to note is the society one the MCs choose to live in or a society that they are doomed to exist in? This can and should be reflected by the character's attitude, revealing which this setting is as well as his or her temperament when dealing with others.

Build the neighborhood community carefully, and it will reap numerous character development details. Privacy needs of the main character are also revealed. Is he or she shy or eagerly involved with all communal activities? Or is he or she an introvert or perhaps a loner filled with stress? Did he or she just return "home" due to grief or a need to rebuild after a fall? In what form does this character's truth reveal itself? How much does your character need? How does that character use that time between one problem and the next? What forms of decompression are used?

There are many things your side characters can reveal:

- Self-assurance, confidence, or secrecy, does your character have it? Is it different in the workplace rather than at home?

- Friends: who and what does the MC choose to let into his or her life? The choices in friends denote facets of the main character's values, the obligations between them imply limitations and financial boundaries.
- Keepers of hidden truths: the past and traumas can be illustrated by friends. Or these "keepers" could be the long-term neighbors or family.
- If there are no older friends, it is a tip off of trauma, being on the run, hiding from the past. Your readers will wonder why, and your book will read as a a flat, two-dimensional product. Make sure these characters are a purposeful narrative choice.
- Kids versus old people: How does you character interact with each can say a lot, for good or bad, especially when no one is around to judge the behavior. How they deal with each reveals much in few words and actions (aka cursing an old person or forgetting them altogether)
- Regarding kids: Can your MC slow down? Does he or she respect the worries and needs of youth or small kids? The age of the children can impact the choices. Does the MC show them as having value?

In *Hometown Cha Cha Cha*, when the female lead stops to deal with the local children's teeth this demonstrates a caring nature when previously she seemed cold and self-absorbed. This behavior surprised me as a viewer. I wondered why is she so lovable with the kids and so cold to others upon meeting them? Why are her barriers down now? To be honest, I wasn't rooting for her in this romance, until I saw this scene. In but a few minutes of screen time I saw facets of her character that were previously unknown to me, and that new character, I liked. Side characters do more to reveal your main characters than a paragraph of description, dialogue, and actions. Plus, it creates credibility and a MC we can invest in.

But how many storylines are too many? AKA, how many storylines and characters can the reader invest in? All characters matter. If you introduce them, don't let them just be cameo appearances. Characters shouldn't slide into the storyline, and our lives, with no purpose. If there is a meaningful thread to your work, these same characters repeat in some form throughout the piece so that it leads to... something. Don't add an "orphan" character, one that shows up for a line or two and then ceases to exist. It makes the reader / viewer feel betrayed. Why should the reader pay attention to any of your characters, their names and problems, if he or she only drops in for a cameo appearance?Are there really any "side" characters in life? Give them something to contribute to the storyline or to reveal about the primary character. Re-insert them from time to time so that learning their names was not a waste of time. Do they really exist in your main character's world? Then they would interact from time to time. If not, don't name them.

Be careful. Sometimes more is just too much. Sure, fantasy readers may enjoy a large cast of characters, legions, in fact. But do not make these additions to the character list simply for volume. If you add a character, make him or her worthwhile. You are lying to your reader if you give them a name or special notice, but that person ultimately doesn't matter to storyline progression or impact the main character in any significant way. No character should exist simply as a plot point. That's lazy writing.

The Village

It starts with the village. Community, as a whole, is a character, and it is in its appeal that has people clamoring for more. The popular drama of *Hometown Cha Cha Cha* is a prime example of community taking center stage. I would venture to say that community was the main character. It was the mayor/main character's interactions with each town member that revealed the facets of his character. The subsequent romance that developed later had less depth and development than the life-long interactions with friends, colleagues, and neighbors, and yet no one in the audience raving about the drama seemed to care. The village matriarch claimed our attention and endeared the main character to the audience in his interactions with her until eventually finding a love interest.

Nowhere can the impact of community be better seen than in *Hometown Cha Cha Cha*. As is the usual formula, we meet the hero or heroine in the opening lines and are immediately transfixed by some dilemma or challenge that they must overcome. But Korean Dramas don't explain the problem in a linear fashion. No, instead we must absorb much of it through interactions with the rest of the cast of characters. The smallest of interactions, at a shop, with a delivery person, or a co-worker reveal tidbits of our main character's personality far more clearly and concisely than the oppressive "descriptive paragraph". Neighbors reveal to us how our hero or heroine lives, are they solitary or a well-valued member of a community? Is someone waiting at home to assist if needed? A childhood friend perhaps? Or is there a rivalry revealed by hostile placement of recycling totes or walled isolation? The neighborhood also quickly reveals in but a moment the financial status of our main character. It answers the question of whether or not he or she is living with a peer or class group or is the main character the odd man out, the anomaly, perhaps sitting on a precipice of being cast out or moving up?

The neighbors in *Hometown Cha Cha Cha*, while not receiving as many lines or screen time, still were an integral key to telling Du Sik's story. These shopkeepers, adoptive grandmother, and even children know and reveal a different facet of the protagonist that was special. For indeed, it is the role we play with others that casts our character. Is he kind to children? Does he respect his elders or take advantage of their weakness? Does he take advantage of those perhaps not as witty as himself? Likewise, how does the peer group measure the main character? Is this someone who is admired or someone only tolerated? All these questions are answered by the village.

Try this out yourself. Want more bang for your written page (buck)? Place a character in a party or crowded environment and rapid-fire characterization is provided without needing words written specifically to do so. Let the others speak for you— and him or her. Much like when a scientist introduces a new specimen to the petri dish, so, too, does the advent of a chatter into a social circle reveal fascinating results. Give it a spin and see what your community can add to the character development.

The Lovable Friend

The comic foil is not defined by gender in K-drama although most of them tend to be male, but that is not a hard fast rule. In *Cinderella and the Four Knights*, I would hazard to say that main character's novelty is a breath of fresh air. The lovable friend or foil can serve as the main character's support team, family, co-worker, friend, or supernatural aid.

The Disappointment

The "disappointment" and his or her baggage can be harvested by the main character and used as an ally or a means of comparison. Juxtaposition of characters always highlights differences and strengths among people and characters. Likewise, the "disappointment" could be a measuring rod for your main character, such as in *Our Unwritten Seoul*.

If your main character is the underdog, comparisons can still be made to a familial social grouping and reveal more character traits. I'm sure we've all experienced the evolution of someone we thought we knew in the company of their family.

This is where the Korean dramas excel. Family and even old friendships are never far in the shadows. The K-dramas understand that we are the sum of our experiences, and that family (even extended or absentee family), leave scars on our souls.

In the case of a higher social ranking, especially when inheritance (other than debt) is an option, birth order and obligation adds another dimension of characterization. It might even be advantageous to draw a character family tree complete with connections and moral disconnects and possibly even grudges.

DEAR MY FRIENDS (2016)

Writer: Noh Hee-kyung (based on a novel by the same writer)
Genre: Drama with comedic elements, ensemble cast
Produced by: Studio Dragon

Dear My Friends is a multigenerational story that follows the main character, Park Wan, as she spends time with her mother's older friends. The elders struggle with infirmities due to old age, fear of the loss of loved ones, and how to retain self and autonomy as they decline. *Dear My Friends* is powerful in its tender handling of the challenges in senior life. The mother/daughter relationship is tumultuous in this drama, but through their shared friendships in the senior group, they grow closer.

Dear My Friends is a poignant tale of fighting for independence and continues the discussion of how does one end a life and under what terms? Likewise, who will be standing at your side, supporting or limiting you? The show clearly illustrates the harsh effects of aging and asks who gets to make those last choices when you or your loved one can no longer advocate for his or herself? These questions include how to live, with whom, and where? The essential question is how do you navigate the end of life with dignity, grace, and honor friendships?

If you have watched any of the popular dramas, you will recognize several of the faces in this stellar cast. With an ensemble cast, this K-drama carries multiple storylines. It is a good study for converging a lot of characters and plot lines in a meaningful way. Each scene uses action and dialogue to quickly characterize each of the players. This story is not only dramatic but contains realistic and relatable storylines.

HOMETOWN CHA CHA CHA (2021)

Writer: Shin Ha-eun
Genre: drama, romance, ensemble story
Produced by: Studio Dragon

Socially and emotionally fragile, Hey-jin, seeks to escape the competitiveness and aggression of city life when she opens a dental clinic in a small village. However, she underestimates the lack of privacy and pressure that connectivity engenders. She soon encounters, Duk-sik, a young man, a seemingly jack of all trades, whose popularity and outgoing nature challenges her comfort levels. Due-sik seems to know everyone as he is employed in several capacities. Eventually viewers learn that behind it all, Duk-sik is in hiding from his former success.

However, at the true center of the drama is the village and its quirky but lovable occupants. The romantic elements of this story really takes a backseat to the personalities of the community members and the connections Duk-sik has with them. It's more of a love story to small towns than anything else, a charming ode to community.

Nothing in this drama happens in a vacuum. Community has

a role in itself. Lovable friend or misfit, each plays a significant and revealing role. More than a cute storyline, it indeed takes a village. This K-drama's success is proven by the influx of tourists arriving after the show's release, each demanding to grab their own experience in a seaside town.

THE UNCANNY COUNTER (2020, SEASON 1)

Writers: Yeo Ji-na, Yoo Seon-dong, Kim Sae-bom
Genre: Fantasy, thriller, mystery, mild horror
Produced by: Studio Dragon

The Counters, people who escaped death due to various circumstances, awaken from their comas with superhuman strength, abilities, and a calling to battle evil spirits that terrorize the living. Fast-paced and filled with thrilling dangers and fantastical mythologies, *The Uncanny Counter* keeps the viewers on the edge of their seats. The Counters are an endearing and unexpected crew of superheroes trying to blend into mortal life when not on an active case. Motive and morality focus this adventurous tale and develops the theme of chosen family and multigenerational relationships of the found family.

It's a dark super-hero story with rich characters who have simple lives when not saving the world. Rich in innovation, mythology, passion, and thrills, this series well-deserves a subsequent season. Powerfully told while still having the emotional nuance and character development we've all come to love and recognize in K-drama, *The Uncanny Counter* develops each core character's backstory, making it a truly exemplary ensemble cast.

Chapter Four

MORAL BOUNDARIES

Morals and boundaries go hand in hand. But what do we, as writers need to address with this topic?

The core component of our characters should be what they believe in, sometimes religiously but most definitely ethically. A character does not have to be religious in any way, but a moral base is still at the crux of what makes us human. If a character is religious, his or her morality will be based on the contents of the holy book or creeds that they adhere to for the sake of said religion. Without a religious background or a rejection of the religion upon which he or she was raised, there are still ethical choices that have been made. The clarifying point being made here is that morality and religion do not have to be tied together.

What we value as humans is partially due to what we think has merit, and in that merit there is judgment. Likewise, we can praise someone for being a go-getter and applaud his achievements while disapproving the sacrifices that he had to make in order to get to that level of success. We are inundated with movies, news reports, and discussions about what it takes to succeed in the modern day world. With that exposure we can even subconsciously respond to whether the choices those people made are met with our approval. With every forward step comes risk and sometimes reward or pain. Our thought processes about what is worth our effort or censure reflects our morality, our sense of good or bad.

To be fully fleshed out human beings you have to include in your character development at least a baseline of morality. In what do they believe? What types of behavior would they shun or reject outright? For what things will he or she fight? And on what modern social issue or problem would they be willing to take a stand and voice an opinion?

K-dramas like to present issues that are contemporary and sometimes debatable. It is in these small scenes that the writer can reveal to the viewer / reader what is most important to the character. In the small choices the bigger issues become clear. For example, in *Rain or Shine* Kang-doo can appear quite tough and independent. He will not concede to others' demands, as quite frankly, he has seen and dealt with enough to have toughened and become cynical. But when his sister has needs that he can fulfill, his desires and preferences take the backseat to doing all he can to fill that need. In his self-sacrifice his morality is exposed. On the flip side, he has no problem engaging in questionable business practices, fighting, or keeping company with others that might seem less that upstanding. The gray areas in his morality and the contrasting characterization as his ethics are situational, produce a more human character. A realistic character, for all his or her flaws, is more enticing than a someone whose boundaries are rigid.

Moral boundaries tests the limits of your characters' values and ethics. Each K-drama's main character must exhibit these moral boundaries to make the character believable, for an example, *Nevertheless* (2021). Labelled as a romance, *Nevertheless* challenges the ideas of dependency and trust. It opens with a horrific realization and develops into an unhealthy coupling of the main characters. What we should and should not do or accept is explored in a realistic manner, thus making the characters' choices that much more poignant and haunting. Much like *My Liberation Notes,* this drama explores the needier side of longing and despair.

In contrast, *Love Next Door* (2024) has a more light-hearted conflict between the characters. These boundaries make the story bloom into something engaging and possibly anxiety-inducing in the viewer / reader. We want to know more than how this will play out. That is where the magic begins, in our anticipation and questioning, much like the characters themselves. Question, doubt, and reach for more. We must do the same as those writers. The audience should be the last person we plan for in order to yield engagement

Morality and Ethics

Everyone has some level of these. If you haven't sorted out your characters' default reactions, your work isn't complete. Studio Dragon's *Little Women* (2022) provides an example of morality at the forefront. These women are not the poster children of traditional purity and piety with humbly bowed heads. In the first episode alone, the valor presented by the main character when faced with injustice, coupled with the desire to correct it, explains much of the character's emotional make-up. She wants to make the guilty accountable. Other moral issues, alcoholism, indebtedness and the accompanying shame and obligation, family loyalty and sacrifice, betrayal, jealousy, and what one could sell or barter for financial gain is presented and weighed. All in episode one. Amazing! It sounds like too much, but rather than leaning towards the overly dramatic and superficial drama, this K-drama reeks of realism and humanity. The result? Full on viewer engagement with the knowledge and anticipation that, in not only one but all of sixteen episodes, there would be more layers and depth that we, the viewers, cannot even surmise.

This is exactly why we, a larger portion of the United States as well as other parts of the world, are enamored and even addicted to Korean Drama. One could easily sit through two or three episodes at a time and still mourn the fact that sleep, work, or other obligation forces us to tear our eyes away for the evening.

Isn't that what you want for your books and your readers? An audience enthralled will always reach for more and the translates into dollars in your pocket.

To do this, there must be a moral stake in your work for the readers to really care. To this end, do the leg work. Test out your character, wherever you are in the process and determine his or her moral baseline. It will make the "real" writing have focus and be more intentional and true to who you've created.

NEVERTHELESS (2021)

Based on a Webtoon: *Nevertheless* written by Jung Seo
Genre: Romance? (If so, it is dependent, manipulative, obsessive)
Produced by: Studio N

Morals and morality are at the heart of this drama. *Nevertheless* opens with a failed and exploitive relationship and continues with further dysfunctional, co-dependent, and yet skeptical lovers. The dark side of attraction and the risks involved in finding true love make this drama both engaging and cringy. The drama delves into the depths of the human heart and its doubts and fears. Realistic and bold, this is not a traditional romance with feel-good montages. However, the drama is well-produced with skilled actors that make the storyline both believable and painful to watch as the main characters in their search to define love. The drama delves into deep issues not suitable for younger audiences.

MY LIBERATION NOTES (2020)

Writer: Park Hae-young
Genre: Drama, family
Produced by: Studio Phoenix; Chorokbaem Media; SLL

The story centers around three siblings who all seek to escape their mundane existence of the family home and business by traveling to Seoul daily for work. Employed in various fields, happiness eludes them, and they remain unfulfilled. The long commute only serves to give them time to think about their failed dreams. They each wallow in depression and personal frustrations making this drama sometimes painful to watch in its skillful depiction of inner turmoil and regret. When a stranger, Mr. Gu, moves into their rental unit, intrigue is added for the youngest daughter who is drawn to his reclusive mannerisms and questionable past morality. Her despair is matched by his own. Powerful and poignant, secrets and the frustrations of the main characters' hopes make this a mesmerizing and soul-touching watch.

LITTLE WOMEN (2022)

Writer: Jeong Seo-kyung
Genre: Mystery, thriller, family drama
Produced by: Studio Dragon

The story follows three sisters whose independent streak and family loyalty are a nod to the original *Little Women* novel by Louisa May Alcott. However, not much else connects the two pieces. Dangerous situations and mystery in which people are not who they first appear to be keeps the viewers on the razor's edge with tension and anticipation. However, these skilled writers keep the audience misled throughout. The oldest sister, In-joo, is the focus of the drama and her search for money to provide the stability her family needs. In-kyung, the second sister, works as a news reporter, intent on finding the truth, no matter the cost. The final sister, In-hye, is an aspiring artist who longs for the opportunity money would provide for her to pursue her dreams of art, fame, and travel, much like the youngest of the original March sisters. However, the similarities to the original namesake novel ends there. Conflicting drives and passions cause the sisters to separate as they chase their individual desires. However, their stories overlap and prove deadly. Each sister is a fully fleshed out character and as endearing as the March girls, perhaps with more edge and grit of the modern day woman. *Little Women* is a powerful update to the original.

THE POTATO LAB (2025)

Writer: Kim Ho-soo
Genre: Romantic Comedy
Produced by: Chorokbaem Media

The Potato Lab is a story of contrasts; an analytical director and a passionate potato researcher butt heads in this Rom-Com.

Hot-headed and unreasonable Kim Mi-kyung's hope for advancement wars with her desire to (literally) plant roots. What was initially a moment of shame and loss when forced to return to her home village turned out to be exactly what she needed to heal from a romance gone wrong and social betrayal.

Cold and calculating, So Baek-ho is just doing what he does best— cutting costs and trimming perceived redundancies in staff. This executive, passing through on a temporary assignment to do what he does regarding acquisitions and efficiency, becomes entangled in a battle of wills between two people who know what they want and believe their way is right.

Often through humorous encounters, both characters experience personal growth and refine perspectives of what matters most. Each learns that they'd underestimated the other, eventually resulting in a business and romantic partnership.

Chapter Five

SETTING

Setting in K-drama is so much more than where. Unlike the cardboard box of a diorama project, the settings are impactful and work as a way to further characterize, restrict, and reveal the main character. These landscapes are not overly contrived but rather backdrops of a good story.

Cities: The vibrancy and pace of the idealized city is not the trope explored in K-drama. Yes, there are the polished finishes and space of the posh city apartment and incredible skyline views (Especially useful for a possible "suicide" as in *Little Women*). The city scape does not only lure travelers (as in *Hometown Cha Cha Cha*'s neighborhood invasion) or in contrast encourage escape to Jeju Island. Likewise, the city serves to provide a contrast in the form of choice, opportunity, or prestige without being heavy-handed.

Countryside: A country home, especially when in juxtaposition against a city job (*The Potato Lab*) is a chance to slow the pace and a prime spot for introspection (such as in *My Liberation Notes*). The pace and limits of a country life is an amalgam of the unrelenting needs and expectations of the land. The routine, too, can be healing or oppressive, drawing forth introspection and expanding the sense of time.

The Vacation: Where people go to escape their normal setting is telling. Do they go camping to "rough it" or to a splurge by the sea or in a hotel (whether easily afforded or not)? When the vacation is a place that harkens back to home, then you have an opportunity for backstory.

A Commoner's Home: Realism is one of the selling points of many K-dramas. The audience's connection to the people or characters depicted is elemental to its ongoing draw. So it is even more important that the homes and apartments do not feel staged or contrived in any way. When you are watching K-drama, you see the ugly plastic containers of kimchi, the worn bed rolls, the cluttered counters, and therefore, feel the strain of want. You see someone scoop out two cups of rice to cook and then put back a half cup after a quick appraisal of the cupboard contents. Small gestures like these are what K-drama has mastered and do not feel contrived; they feel refreshingly human. And that humanity is what all writers should strive for.

The setting is a monetary and social classification of the life your character lives. It is, perhaps, the most voyeuristic element of the K-drama— an intimate peek into someone's home. I wonder, perhaps, if these are not staged but filmed in people's homes as the immersion is perfect. The authenticity, however they manage it, furthers the illusion and investment of the viewer / audience.

Set Dressing

Time period and caste should be revealed through living arrangements. For set dressing, think immersion. Many of us became writers because we wondered "what if?" But "what if" needs context. If the reader (or viewer) is to follow our thought process, we must leave the breadcrumbs. In *It's Okay Not to Be Okay*, we, the viewers, needed more than exposition to see the main characters' traumas. At one point in the series a spirit is suspended over the main character's body, terrorizing Moon-Young's sleep in her lush childhood bedroom. In another scene, the drawings in her book are animated to express inner turmoil. Emotional scene setting is a thing, too. Add details, right down to the brand of alcohol or beer they drink to further characterize. *Start Up* (2020) has a quick insight to how the guys had been living and their sacrifices. The dingy apartment, studio area, shared experiences, and worries did much to depict social class and their need for advancement.

A Rich Back Story

There are several rules to developing this:

1. Block the setting— everyone is somewhere and purposely
2. When you use symbols, repeat them and make them purposeful
3. Time honored mythology should be respected and at least addressed if changed
4. Plot devices— don't be hokey
5. Create a rich friend circle

Setting is like a character in itself. It provides the context. It needs to be introduced in fragments as needed. Its purpose is to increase the stakes, intrigue, and depth of complex relationships. A year and place designation is enough of a start for fantasy of historical context. The rest can wait.

Where and when sets the limitations for the storyline as well as the characters. For example, in *Hometown Cha Cha Cha* setting took on a life of its own, to the point that the Korean government has to plea with viewers and fans of the show to stop visiting the small coastal town as the people who actually lived in the popular drama's key filming locations could not go about their lives long after the show wrapped. The setting was so well-utilized that the viewers felt an attachment to the place as much as they would a main character, forgetting, perhaps that the setting was packaged in a way that made the story work and not an absolute representation of the place. Hoards and hoards of fans besieged the village with their cameras and loved ones to glean and claim a small portion of the warmth the setting provided. While *Hometown Cha Cha Cha*'s draw wasn't strictly the vistas but the extended warmth exuded by the ensemble cast, it was the setting that drove tourists to select this as as their destination, swelling the economy and daily commuting woes.

The mournful coast and limited housing and work options created the boundaries of this drama. So, too, the author must think out fully where would my story best be told? How will the natural environment enhance the emotion of my key players? Where would there be boundaries? When I reference boundaries I am not speaking in a literal way but rather social, economic, and cultural.

Setting is as much about personal restrictions as it is about topography. A poor character must exist within his or her environ and adapt rather than have the luxury of movement. Movement between locations, opportunities, obligation (both familial and cultural) unfortunately are often the prerogative of only the monied. These are the decisions that the author must make early in the drafting stage. A clearly defined or envisaged setting will help guide the formation of the character and his or her character when faced with choice.

Which should you develop first, the setting or the character? I honestly believe it depends on where your inspiration sparked. Was it a character that whispered into your ear, begging you to tell his story? Or was it a time period or an artifact that began the nagging sensation of a story percolating? Honor the spark. Wherever the root of your muse, start there. Then expand out to create the setting or to place the character into the context of a known (at least to you) locale. Delineate the limitations and benefits. Include things like: the season, dates (year, month, days even), and specify at least a few landmarks. Landmarks might only include the main character's home or apartment at the start, but consider, too, where does he shop or she get her hair done? How far is work from home? Does he have to hitch a ride or drive a hybrid car or sports car? Does she ride the bus to get a lux manicure or does she walk to save the car fare perhaps indicating vanity over inconvenience. Does he attend the local community college or is she far from a populated area and therefore limited in her choices? Setting often defines the characters' reach and growth possibilities.

In *Our Unwritten Seoul*, setting is the primary focus. One sister gets freedom and the pressures of the city and the other twin is limited by small town options, creating vastly different lives.

CRASH LANDING ON YOU (2020)

Writer: Park Ji-eun
Genre: Historical Romantic / Drama
Released by: Studio Dragon

Blown off course while paragliding, Se-ri finds herself in the DMZ of North Korea. A captain of the People's Republic Army, Jeong-hyeok is the first to find her and decides to help her evade arrest by the government. In doing so, he risks his career, status, and possible freedom— because he know the risks for her include jail and possible prison time. He plans to help her cross the border before detection. Unfortunately, his decision to intervene in her possible capture risks his comrades. The loyalty of friendship and a subtly blossoming romance as time passes makes this all the more complicated. *Crash Landing on You* juxtapositions the living standards, societal rules, and values of two people from radically diverse backgrounds. Ultimately, the main characters' personal values lead to a love that defies boundaries.

Crash Landing on You is more than a story about the where and when of the setting; it is socially and culturally tied. For the viewers to escape into this storyline, they must first be immersed in the storyline. Believability through responsible research is key for reliable storytelling.

The clothing, tools, mannerisms, and behaviors are anchored to the time of each opposing reality. Gender roles are also bound by when, where, and distinct social groupings. Even the speech patterns and vocabulary are shaped by time.

The writer explains the limits of the two main protagonists and clearly defines their ability to dream as well as what is obtainable or possible based on each society's limits. Needs are likewise defined by culture. Character motivation and desires are clearly defined.

How can you apply this? Think on the following questions: How far can your protagonist dream? What is obtainable? What is possible based on his or her society? What are the limits of your setting? What is possible is defined by the rules of the society. Likewise you need to define the personal why's for each character to move the story along.

While at the base a character can be good, driven, and/or a dreamer, the scope of each is defined by the limits of the setting. Opportunity is a matter of what options are available.

Crash Landing on You, part 1, reveals just enough details about the main characters to make you care while building suspense. We, the viewers, learn about the characters much like some would learn about a stranger, slowly and over time. The genius move in this drama is that the several moments of character insight and plot twists are things not anticipated by the other POV characters. These revelations both complicate and thrill, adding more suspense. Each new bit of information builds the suspense which further engages the viewer since we have now vested with the main characters and their literal boundaries.

Chapter Six

SOCIAL SETTING

One of the biggest mistakes that new writers make is when they create a character in a vacuum. No one and nothing can exist in a vacuum. Period. The simple truth is, that in the absence of air, all things die. This is true of our stories as well.

Characters need other characters to grow, to feed upon, to react to, learn from, be inspired by, to envy, and to love. The list can go on for days. But alone, the character can only wallow in the past or fear the future. This doesn't mean that you should create someone simply to have dialogue with a two dimensional character to simply spout your backstory to... NO!

Often when we write we think what is my character doing? What will he or she say? And then we craft stories and plotlines specifically to move our character's growth, but that is as far from life as possible, and as such, will not maintain a following. The best TV series of the last several decades had ensemble casts: *Mash, Friends, Seinfeld, Gilmore Girls, ER*. Yes, there were characters that took the lead role, but it is in the community that our hero or heroine soars.

Who we are as people is the culmination of the people we interacted with, who harmed or scarred us, and experienced life with for however many years we have existed on this planet. To do otherwise with the characters we create would mean we have birthed wooden characters that no one will ever truly engage with— and no stakes means no impact.

Previously, we have all read or viewed rich characters whose misfortune or death made our hearts break and shed a tear. The question is why? What made that character stand out and mean something to us? We all know we are dealing with fiction, and yet, this character has jumped off the page and into our hearts because we believe we know him or her. How does that happen, truly?

Social Setting

Everywhere in Korean Drama, it cannot help but indicate status and money. As a culture rich with tradition, polite social graces, and familial expectation, it is a topic that cannot be avoided in its entirety. The reality is social standing is an underlying current that shapes action, opportunity, and can be a major stressor.

While American drama does note status and money, it usually does so by the choice of car, home, designer clothing, and the occasional man left out of plans. It illustrates status in the moment. This is not so in K-drama.

Korean Drama reveals the ingrained behavior as the result of caste that imbeds to the bone. This belief shapes the confidence, opportunity, and friendships, yielding layers of impact. Sometimes the juxtaposition of the haves and the have-nots is presented in an extreme and pointed manner, but most often it is revealed in a more subtle framework. The benefit of this is that when such things are accepted simply as the way of things, the character no longer fights against the tide but rather is shaped by constant erosive nature of living in such a way for long periods of time. The character is found lacking in some way by the others or self-assesses to be so. This helps the script writers build characters that are not only more relatable but layered and complicated amalgams of fate and choice within their limitations. One such drama is *Celebrity*; it explores the life of an influencer and the rapid rise to fame and money as well as the pitfalls of bowing to the need to constantly prove oneself. These roles are clearly illustrated.

Complex Family Dramas and Interconnectivity

For the sake of POV we often write with a narrow perspective. This can be powerful and serve to draw not only the reader in but supports connection and believability. In newer writers, other characters serve as plot movers, but Korean Dramas build multiple plot lines. The family dynamic, while secondary in many stories, has a backstory and nuance that one should not be able to "read" overnight, with motives unique to the individuals and family. K-drama proves that you can have a dynamic protagonist and yet incorporate secondary characters in a way that is not self-serving or one dimensional. Their secondary characters' plot lines often go unsolved, as they should be. They are not the narrative focus. These are not left as "hanging threads", incomplete in total, but are at least leading in a direction so as to satisfy even the most critical audience. Realistically, our problems do not sync up when our friends' do. But the richness that these characters provide is key to a believable protagonist and rich world building, such as 2024's *Love Next Door* by Studio Dragon.

Like in any drama, family serves as a frame for disfunction and childhood trauma. For a good reference, view the K-dramas, *Little Women, Love Next Door, My Unfamiliar Family,* and *My Liberation Notes*. However, in Korean dramas, family is very much a hierarchy. It couldn't hurt to think of your characters' families like this as well.

Things to consider include:

- Whose word has the most influence on your main characters?
- Who is the champion of emotional drama?
- Who is neglectful?
- Who wields the most control?
- Who gets "shorted" in the family? (Neglected, or overlooked).
- Who makes the final decisions? Whose word is "law"?
- Who is the disappointment in the family? (There usually is one.)

Korean Drama makes sure to define rules of the culture in a piece, by time or fantastical setting. The rules sometimes make the reader and viewer uncomfortable, and perhaps that is the point. Rules include: social-economic status, sexuality, gender limits imposed by society on men versus women (such as *Crash Landing on You* with the differences between North and South Korea forefront).

Other sets of rules include:

- Spiritual rules as in *The Hotel Del Luna*
- Cultural rules as in *Because This is My First Life*
- Social rules *Run On*
- Financial advantage in *My Demon*
- Social expectation in *Crash Landing on You*
- Mystical rules as in *The Uncanny Counter*

Rules of Culture

Part of the international draw to K-drama is that the cultural boundaries are clearly defined in action, dialogue, and patterns. As in any fantasy or science fiction piece, you have to know the rules of your world and the literal and metaphysical boundaries of your map. This general rule works equally well for corporate scenes, families, and friend groups. Within the first episode or two the boundaries (real or perceived) and expectations of your main character should be clear. This especially helps new K-drama viewers who are now essentially readers (as we read in translation) anchor our expectations so that we can connect on a human level, the level of engagement. These rules define the character's behavior and options.

Spiritual rules are defined by the religion or mythology employed. An example of spatial rules can be found in *The Uncanny Counter* or *Hotel del Luna*. Some of these rules include what constitutes "passing over" to death, what Death looks like in personified form, who can see the dead, and what anchors those who have not crossed over. Having these rules in place help make even the most fantastical story feel logical and structures character actions. Understanding these rules helps the readers or viewers anticipate and ponder with their beloved characters.

Social rules include things we all have experienced within our modern world. However, these rules need defining for the sake of the context of the story to ground your audience. Employment advantage or bias, dominant role in marriage, step family or second family, gender limitations, imbalances of opportunity etc. Rules do not have to be concrete or across the whole society, but they must define what is true for the character's time period, context, and environment.

Rules create a margin of trust that breaks international and language barriers. If the framework is clear, the reader can trust the storytelling and anticipate with the main character. It is in understanding these rules that we can anticipate and deepen our empathy with the main character. However, there are a couple of rules romance writers must abide by. Someone does get the girl, and the right couple ends up together with a happily ever after. If the romance does not tie up in this manner, it cannot be labelled as such.

Social Behavior

Symbolism is everywhere and not just in tattoos (largely western) and religious symbols. They exist in clothing brands and cars. Even cell phones and alcohol indicate caste, class, and monetary level. Aside from these obvious indicators, signs and symbolism toward building interconnectivity between characters are rampant if you are attentive enough to notice. These include:

Religions are filled with common tropes and patterns are capitalized on and work well here. Mythological religious entities are also explored, such as the frequent personification of the Grim Reaper (in his many shapes and forms) and the prevalence of assorted deities as needed. Meanwhile, evil spirits are presented in their commonly accepted stereotypes.

Relationships naturally occur between friends, coworkers, family, and love interests. There are also overlapping social groups. Sometimes our social groups are independent of each other. Other times they naturally overlap. (Ie: children's extra curricular activities where co-workers find another with something in common and connect). These relationships expose us to a bigger world picture such as politics, social class, and the caste-like impact of chosen career fields.

Funeral rites, the how we mourn and where we mourn, reveals much of what a character values or how he or she is valued once deceased. The food memorial rites can be indicated by a simple placard on a wall, a reserved hall and meal, a funeral well-attended... or not. All serve to characterize and socially set our story. Memorial food can be basic or opulent, a tedious yearly rite or a celebration of a life well-lived, or perhaps, frequently forgotten.

A simpler example of interconnectivity can be in the common act of making of kimchi. It can be a family obligation such as in *Because This Is My First Life* or a symbolic gift of love and caring, a sign of thoughtfulness as in *Miss Day and Night*.

The act of drinking, be it socially or as part of a business event, has layered meanings. When to drink, what to drink, and who you drink with, all matters. There are specific manners required when drinking with peers versus employers or co-workers. Who is deferred to and the type of beverage reveals caste, class, and levels of social order and respect. Do you turn your head away and cover your mouth while drinking as a sign of deference? Who pours for whom? Perhaps each pour for the other. This is yet another convention of a culture represented by action and tells the audience much with few words.

Watch with a tourist's eye as you view any Korean Drama, and you find much being said between the lines with simple actions and yet a clear structure of social behavior.

CINDERELLA AND THE FOUR KNIGHTS (2016)

Based on web novel of the same name

Writers: Min Ji-eun and Won Young-sil
Genre: Rom-Com, family drama, ensemble cast
Produces by: Studio Dragon

Cinderella and the Four Knights, complete with an evil stepmother and stepsister, turns the traditional fairy tale on its end. Instead of being a woman in need of rescue, Eun Ha-won may just be the three male leads' salvation.

Powerful Chairman Kang of seemingly endless wealth needs a level head to tame his three grandsons. He terms his heirs simply as a "playboy", an untamable "thug", and a "loser". However, the three turn out to be far more than first appearances would indicate. It's up to Ha-won to help the chairman and themselves to see behind the facades in order to form a family. (The fourth knight I won't spoil for you.)

Family traumas and grief shape the character of these young men and is so deeply ingrained into their response to the world that it will take a miracle to change their trajectory. With humor and heart, Studio Dragon uses the *Cinderella* tale as a frame for this charming and often heartbreaking story of a family divided.

EXTRAORDINARY ATTORNEY WOO (2022)

Writer: Moon Ji-won
Genre: Drama
Produced by: AStory, KT Studio Genie, Nangman Crew

The drama follows Woo Young-woo as she navigates the confusion of becoming a rookie attorney at a prestigious law firm. This is especially challenging as her autism manifests in ticks and odd coping mechanisms that are impossible to ignore. Young-woo struggles with common social clues, but her unique way of looking at the world lets her see what others miss. What's special about this K-drama isn't just that the lead is neurodivergent; it's how the camera reveals her thought processing so that we, the viewer, can follow where her mind leads. Young-woo's weaknesses are also her strengths, eventually drawing the romantic interest of a co-worker who appreciates Young-woo just as she is. Charming and bittersweet at times, *Extraordinary Attorney Woo* is endearing in its resilience and brilliant character development.

MY UNFAMILIAR FAMILY (2020)

Written by Kim Eun-jung
Genre: Drama
Produced by: Studio Dragon

My Unfamiliar Family opens on Eun-hee, a frazzled and overworked employee. Within the first few moments we see a broken family that has more grievances with each other than open conversation. Three grown siblings, one a doctor's wife, a minimally employed younger son, and the stressed office worker, are all so absorbed in their own lives and perceived slights that they miss their father's struggles with memory.

Dysfunctional relationships are compounded by misunderstandings and long-hidden secrets make this drama stark with its bitter reality and tough calls. At times the characters are aggressive in their animosity, and at other times the characterization is subtle, guided by small moments and pangs of longing. Well-balanced with a powerful ensemble cast, this drama proves that no character should be underdeveloped but rather built to enhance the core storyline.

Chapter Seven

A SATISFYING STORY ARC

A believable storyline is seldom simple. It is more of a tangled knot, because life isn't linear, not if you really think about it. When has anything gone to plan? Unlike American drama that goes from point A to B to C (partially due to time constraints with all those televised commercials) K-drama's meandering path to the conclusion provides opportunity for plot twists, false starts and failures, and redirection— AKA how life really is.

All the choices that people make in the real world are complicated by expectation, obligation, anticipated reactions from family and others, and the baggage that we tow along in life. Or maybe the main character doesn't know what he or she wants in life? Then life is a more of a puzzling maze with an exploration of dead ends and options. Regardless of the life, each main character deserves a satisfying story arc that is well-planned and has depth of development.

The Twist

When a twist arrives, angst can be increased, viewer or reader interest is renewed, and further emotional investment from your audience can take place. Examples include:

The Unexpected or Unwelcome Guest: This person is upsetting to one of the primary characters for some yet undisclosed reason. Tension mounts, and viewers sit closer to the television set or computer screen, intrigued and fearful of how this will impact the story and their hope for a happily ever after for those deserving. This new character undoubtedly brings with him or herself information previously unknown the the audience, a secret that must be handled, or a bit of new drama that will ultimately test and reveal more of the main character for good or ill. This character serves as the skeleton in the closet that suddenly awakens to add layers to the main character you *thought* you knew so well. (For example, see *My Liberation Notes*).

The Threat of Financial Ruin or a Familial Obligation: It interrupts the desires of the main character or characters to either foil the forward progression to their dreams or to foist guilt and remorse onto their psyche. This ultimately confounds the character from making progress toward his or her goals in a way that makes the viewer or reader "root" for the character. Key to this being a successful turn, this element or obligation is relatable to audiences regardless of the situational specifics. It is a relatable situation that most people contend with and have to balance in their own lives.

A Past Promise Revealed: This is a different level of obligation. It could be a promise to oneself, a dying parent, a pact with a friend, a debt for a prior concession, or a romantic entanglement, but ultimately, it is a peek into the character's history that would not normally be revealed in normal interactions with others. The promise is intimate to who and what the character believes in and can reveal an element of his or her moral compass or lack thereof.

All these items reveal more of the primary character, such as: his or her tenacity in the wake of sometimes unreasonable odds, whether he or she has a fight or flight instinct, who does the MC go to for help, and does the character verbalize or withhold? (An example would be Gang-tae's obligation for Sang-tae in *It's Okay Not to Be Okay 2020*).

Explore the possibility of a twist or curve ball. You do not have to include it in your storyline for the practice to have impact. Even if the twist doesn't ultimately occur in the novel or short story, it helps you understand your character and reveal what you see and inherently believe about your character. Place your character in a simple test, what would my character do if he was a child of dying parents? What if a friend's dog was in a burning building, what would the reaction be? Or perhaps she is charged with a crime due to a mistaken identity.

K-dramas excel at twists, often surprising ones. And each time we, the audience, gain more insight into the character and the story's stakes. If couldn't hurt to explore some options in your own story. Whether the result is used in your work or not, what the twist will reveal about your character to you through this quest can help you build depth.

The Curve Ball

Undoubtedly, after you have become attached to your characters and invested in the storyline, the Korean Drama will toss in yet another "Curve ball". The Curve Ball is a type of plot twist or newly revealed info that changes perception and expands the backstory. It triggers movement, decisions, and sometimes panic. It can also up the stakes for your readers and increase the urgency, stress, engagement, and connection. The reader or viewer is very much a part of the equation of a successful story. Keep them rooting for your characters, and they are liable to recommend your book to others as the emotional tug earned staying power in their hearts and minds. Don't you just love a story that wasn't predictable? Especially one that kept you thinking long after the last word was read?

You may have thought the initial hook, with it's enticing and sometimes angst-inducing opening scenes, that your storyline was mapped out. This emotional response applies to both the viewer as well as the main characters. While it is true that thought carried you through several hours, if not several episodes of the series, that main storyline was never going to continue uninterrupted until a happily ever after— at least for most. Life simply isn't like that, and for your readers to truly invest in your words, there needs to be something new to sustain the stakes (both emotionally and physically.)

Similar to an unexpected wall in a maze, the plot twist demands a reaction, a choice for the character. Through the Curve Ball, we get to see the character's thought process, his or her ability to adapt, or not, and his or her reasoning, whether it be in panic-mode or pragmatic. Much can be learned in a small space of time with a Curve Ball while also providing depth of character development.

If the Curve Ball is unraveling without the main character's knowledge, it can also increase suspense, reader tension, and cause side characters to react in anticipation of the main character's reaction. This can provide opportunities for humor or empathy depending on the tone of your writing. These preliminary responses for any of the characters can be misleading or highlight the responses we do eventually get from the main character... or it could be a set up for a further change. The options are endless while also potentially providing a high yield.

The Slowdown

Likewise, sometimes the plot seems to progress too quickly with all the side characters, misunderstandings, plot twists, and surprises. In *Heavenly Ever After* (2025) the main character's social and emotional growth is slow in comparison to everything that is going on around her with so many rules to learn and situations to explore. In the magnificent world building and culture of *Heavenly Ever After*, Hae-sook is slow to adapt. Considering the main character has entered a new reality, Heaven, the pacing of her evolution not only makes sense, it serves to facilitate the audience's growth and discovery as well. In careful plotting, the writers considered their audience and how to bring them along and experience the world with Hae-sook. However, if one were to step back and look at the main character's progress only, she seems almost stagnant, like a pawn on the chessboard, taking one, slow, step at a time. In the case of this storyline, this purposeful plotting choice actually fosters more connection. We, the audience, get to experience with her the subtleties that lead to her acceptance of this new reality. Other characters with similar, slow progression are found in The *Extraordinary Attorney Woo (2022)* and *Because This Is My First Life* (2017).

Additional plot lines divert the viewer from the fact that the main character, by comparison, hasn't progressed much physically or emotionally. What these side quests and characters are actually doing is allowing the main character to ponder, wallow, and/or reflect. All of which garners deeper emotional appeal with the audience and depth of reasoning to satisfy the most discerning. By degrees, we find ourselves investing much more into the main character's plight. He or she is revealed organically, over a crafty trick of time as true friendships would be built in the real world. What the K-drama writers have done is actuality create a slight-of-hand trick, like the cup game. While you are watching the evolution of all around the main character, you've lost sight of the ball, drawn by the shuffle of the cups, and as we relax our guard. Small measured progress inches forward, minuscule while precise. However, cast into the periphery, it feels less forced and linear than most American dramas, and that realism makes us believe.

When a writer can make you invest emotionally, especially in a fictional setting or outright fantasy, they have succeeded in changing words into magic. These writers have created a complete and convincing world, unraveling before the eyes of its viewers/ readers, and drawing us, entranced, toward its climax or resolution.

The Misunderstanding

The misunderstanding can be one of the most enjoyable or torturous plot line, largely because the audience is included in the mistake long before the characters are. The audience has seen the clues as well as what the other characters have been up to when the main character is not in frame. As a result, the audience may want to scream, yell, or otherwise let the hero and/or heroine know that they've made a possibly catastrophic match, but that isn't possible.

The misunderstanding is a huge trope with Korean Dramas, and while predictable, it does cause time to slow as characters reflect on this new fallout of the plot. Perhaps the lesson here is simply to slow down and examine all angles of the current storyline. Where are the holes or gaps in narration? And how would our key players or main character react? Exploring this makes for a simple plot twist.

Two Worlds

In a story of two worlds, such as in *Crash Landing on You*, the contrasts are sharp and clear while some issues overlap with grace and sentimentality. The clashes are not for the sake of contrast but for plot development and to present stakes and obstacles. Clear parameters of what is at stake, as well as defined limits that do not happen conveniently "because plot", keep the readers' / viewers' trust even when presenting an insurmountable problem. Much of life and the best art is immersive. To successfully achieve this, research is key. Research the time period and historical events that will serve as timeline anchors: the slang of the day, popular music, and food. Don't forget to note the gender rules, roles, and limits. If you are breaking the rules with your writing, make it clear that you are.

A Satisfying Payout

After building up tension, trauma, and suspense, the audience expects a payout, and that is what K-drama does with skill. One of the reasons viewers connect to K-drama is that the expectation of a satisfying resolution is always fulfilled. This doesn't mean the terminal patient (as in *Thirty-Nine)* or the elderly matriarch will escape death, (as in *Hometown Cha Cha Cha* or *Dear My Friends)* but rather that life will resolve with some level of hope for those who remain behind. It also does not mean that tension is removed because of an anticipated satisfying happy ending. However, every plot thread is considered, not simply tied up neatly. There are surprises up until the finale. If everything were predictably plotted, why would anyone turn in each week? That is also the thought you need to consider at the end of each and every chapter that you write. Why should the reader continue? An ending is never going to satisfy the reader or viewer if he or she can predict it well before the conclusion. Likewise, if there is no tension or stakes, the ending will never fulfill. We (readers and viewers) want to root for the characters, and we can't do that if we don't care about them or if the plotting is lazy and predictable. So, yes, tug on the heartstrings, just don't tie it all neatly in a bow. For example, in *Crash Landing on You*, I couldn't have predicted the solution to what seemed to be insolvable social and political issues. The writers didn't "magic" a solution, but rather they came up with a well-reasoned and believable conclusion.

Even the minor characters you write should have subplots that are planned, rewarding the viewer's interest and investment in them. Perhaps you should think of the reader/viewer as a relationship that has invested time and their emotions. The lesson here is that if you add side characters (and who lives in isolation?) then make their lives matter, too. They are not simply a plot device, or at least they shouldn't be if you want a three dimensional story. So as you plot, make sure you pull the threads of not only the main characters but all the secondary plots (as in *Start Up*) that matter to the feel and scope of the story. For example, in *Hotel Del Luna*, each of the main characters at the hotel got their story (or grudge) resolved— somehow. Some endings are bittersweet and others just a relief from life's challenges or tests are completed. The end payout needs to ultimately satisfy the emotional stakes.

How many storylines are too many? How many characters can the reader reasonably invest in? I think the simple answer to that is you have a central character (or two) whose story arc you are building. Include the storylines that interact in a meaningful way. Ask yourself, the creator, do these companion stories enrich the character development and growth of your primary character? Or does this extra path lead you away from the main story you wish to tell? *Dear My Friends* (2016) found the perfect balance. Each character and friendship enhanced the other storylines until the main character became more of a hub, a central connecting point, than the sole focus. Likewise, in *Little Women* (2022) and *Start Up* (2020) the intertwining storylines added to each main character rather than detracted.

Companion stories should add interest and dimension to your main players. A secondary storyline can add movement while your main characters need time to deal with the minutia of their own evolution. It becomes too much when the secondary plot line spins out into a new dimension unrelated to the main. Ask yourself, what does developing this additional plot line add? If nothing, cut it. If it builds to the point of overshadowing the main story or possibly building into a new novel altogether, you have to determine where your priorities lie. It could be you have a second novel emerging, and that plot line needs to be cut free from your primary project to be developed on its own. (This is not to say you couldn't have a spin off possibility here. But if you have enough for a whole new novel, trim this secondary to only what is needed for this primary tale and shift the excess files into a new folder for later development.)

Battling Writer's Block

As you explore your character, throw in "what ifs" to test what you know about your character to be true. This is especially useful when you hit a stage of writer's block. For example, you don't know whether character A should take a promotion and move away from character B. Step outside of your story, and this is key. Change time period, place, situation, and throw in a collapsed wall due to a natural disaster (Such as in *Rain or Shine*), find out that upon the death of a parent that the business you thought you would inherit (as is *Do,Do Sol Sol La La So* 2020) is overdrawn and being seized by debtors, or kill off a pet (just not really in a book or your readers will hate you forever) but do so in your side exploration. It will reveal your character's true commitment level and connection, how they deal with grief, etc. Take them on an absurd journey, such as on the back of a flying dinosaur. (Not that that wouldn't be fun). But a fifteen minute exercise where you take your characters out their comfort zones will reveal whether they stretch forward in anticipation and excitement at a new challenge or hide behind a rock, cover their heads, whimpering or pretend the scary situation isn't there at all.

Change it up. These exercises will reveal to you what you do not even consciously know about your character but will force your exploration. The more your know about their motivations and reactions, the better you'll be able to flesh out your interactions as they appear in your novel. Plus, inconsistency in character development, or worse yet, a feeling of betrayal as in "Oh, no, character X would never have done that!" will kill audience loyalty and most likely prevent the reader from returning to your writing at a future date. Better to find out now who your characters truly is. (See *Little Women* for constant twists and how the characters react.)

Create a chart and test your character out. For example, create a twist list and then hypothesize a reaction.

1. Character loses all his or her money, job, or family. What does he or she do next?
2. Character gets a substantial inheritance. Does he or she share, splurge, or save?
3. Something important that was expected doesn't arrive. What does that change?
4. Character is forced to move. Why? And now what?

HEAVENLY EVER AFTER (2025)

Writers: Lee Nam-kyu and Kim Su-jin
Genre: Fantasy drama, comedic elements
Produced by: Studio Phoenix

Heavenly Ever After opens with an elderly loan shark, Lee Hae-sook, exacting payment. Forced into the business by debt and a need to support her bedridden husband, Hae-sook's morals are complicated at best. Not long after her husband passes, Hae-sook dies and manages to slip into heaven. The fantastical setting includes extensive world building and social structure. When being processed by one of heaven's gatekeepers, she is posed the question of what age she'd like be for all eternity. However, upon thinking of her husband's recent comment that she was most beautiful to him just before his death, she chooses to remain an octogenarian. She soon learns she made the wrong choice upon being reunited with her husband, now appearing as he had in his prime. In this brutal and yet comedic turn of events, their odd coupling turns out to be the least of their problems as Hae-sook must face her past demons to earn a place in heaven.

There are several strengths to *Heavenly Ever After*. There is extensive backstory imbedded with characters with clearly defined roles and established rules. The secondary characters move the plot forward in a meaningful way, and emotional heart strings are tugged and in surprising manners. The drama is innovative, even exploring the world through pets' point of view (I hadn't seen that before or with that depth). The main character has more than one inciting incident so that we can see her growth as well as keeping the viewer engaged. Motives are revealed early on and maintained. These shape every action and reaction. The storyline provides numerous ethical and social dilemmas. Internal dialogue is playfully used and is both a key indicator of the main character's emotional state and not so private thoughts, yielding mixed and often amusing reaction from the other characters.

START UP (2020)

Writer: Park Hye-ryun
Genre: Drama, ensemble cast
Produced by: Studio Dragon

Set in the Korean equivalent to Silicon Valley, *Start Up* is a series that explores tech start-up companies' formation and the relationships, financing, and creativity necessary to get to the top. Relationships, both friendly and sibling, are tested as competition for coveted spots with a tech-mentoring collective, Sandbox. An ensemble cast keeps the story from experiencing any lag with its multiple yet intertwining storylines. The characters are vibrant, driven, and have fully fleshed out individual stories, making this a success on many levels.

Emotions run high as so much is at stake for each of the main characters (and there are several). Rich back stories make the viewers emotionally invest in their success. A tech origin story with heart, this K-drama has a solid basis in reality and presents the high stakes of being innovative and first in a business that shifts quickly.

Chapter Eight

EMOTIONAL HEARTSTRINGS

In the opening to the K-drama *Thirty-Nine (39)*, an orphan girl is invited to be adopted by the visiting family from which she had been enjoying the company of their daughter. Instead of a joyous, happy beginning, the child cries and shakes her head. Tears run down her face as she says, "No". The effects of this behavior is surprise, and better yet, curiosity. The viewer is forced to ask, why? After the demonstrative protests, the prospective adoptive parent states, "Of course you want to come home". This is responded to with the following line "For how many nights?"

In those four words we have pages and pages of backstory revealed, and the viewer quickly learns it didn't end well. We know she has been:

Adopted before

She had been returned

And it's happened more than once

How did we know this? It was in the shake of the head, the lone tear, and a face without hope. No yearning glance. No "Really? Maybe?"

The child just busily continues with what she was doing, not even making eye contact with the family.

Few words, purposeful actions, equals big impact. Don't underestimate your audience with telling; instead, let a few actions and words carry the story. Allow your characters' words to breathe, and your audience will get there.

Winning Romance

K-drama knows that for a powerful and engaging romance, the courtship is not perfect.

Usually there is an obstacle, or many, to be overcome. These could be a self-inflicted emotional obstacle, an issue of class or caste etc. They are sometimes "ill-fated" and thus gives us something to root for. Most importantly it isn't predictable or even expected.

Numerous dramas could be noted here. However, I would suggest *Business Proposal*. This drama doesn't present anything that is earthshakingly dramatic. It is in its realism and subtlety that the writer (as a viewer) would be able to note most of the characterization tricks noted earlier. We can also observe a slow burn romance that the audience knows is building, but the couple simply can't seem to get there. The starts and stops in their social progress is both frustrating and lovely. As a result the story lingers with you long after the last frame.

(Purposeful) Lapse in History

The absence of events in a character's history is a tool to provide depth in character, mystery, and something the savvy viewer/reader will want to account for. They, the readers / viewers will lean into the tale, waiting for the void to be filled, often teasingly slow. Prior to the tear-inducing scene in *Thirty-Nine*, we'd seen a montage of the biological child of the prospective adoptive parents coming to the window, much like one would a window in the pet store. All seemed excited at the interactions between the children until the offer to become family. The orphan notices the excited behavior of the others but does not fulfill the emotion that is sought. This takes the viewer back to the universal truth that a dog long left in a kennel in the harsh and sterile environment results in the subsequent learned apathy. It's a trope because it is recognizable, but it is also effective in denoting a lot in a short space of time. A small scene with a big impact, it is a prime example of measured, purposeful writing.

So how do we use this in our own writing? And do we want that kind of speed in development? We all know that speed is needed in the first page, the first ten pages, the first chapter— to hook and engage the reader (or acquisition editor, agent, or publisher). We need speed for the back blurb. We need a pithy and speedy words for the elevator pitch.

When we use tropes to help with speed in communication with our audience, we need to connect clearly and make sure to add why it matters to our character. Personalize the character development so it doesn't feel old, staid, overdone, or worse yet, repetitive. Yes, your audience will recognize the trope, but what makes it new again is in your hands. Remember, it is a basis, a foundation, for what is to come only, not the solution or end game. Part of the enjoyment is K-dramas keep something back, a surprise for later, and just when you think you have it solved, something changes. A trope is a tool, not a destination.

Trauma

The question you have to ask yourself when introducing trauma into your tale is, is it needed or gratuitous? Introducing your characters to trauma can be revealing, move the plot along, and incite action. But is that all it is, a plot device? If so, it is a weak way to develop growth. This is not true for Korean drama. These writers believe trauma, when used, should be purposeful and orchestrated to reveal more depth of character as personal social truths reveal themselves.

What K-drama knows is that the trauma need not be be huge (aka DC's Batman's parents' murder). It could be something smaller, perhaps something seen that might be misperceived or create doubt within a budding relationship. When a character feels doubt, it can create a shaky personal foundation which will impact the choices the character makes or the lack of action, such as hesitation caused by second-guessing. And we all know how missed opportunities can cause lingering regret. Hesitant forward movement, decision-making fumbles, or avoidance altogether, not only add drama but reveal deeper character traits, such as in *Our Unwritten Seoul* (2025).

Trauma is not something you touch and leave. It pervades mannerisms, manifests in body twitches, it cues avoidance behaviors, limits friendship, confounds and complicates familial relationships. It can ripple into complications with work partnerships, romance, or cause break ups. It limits choices and movement, both internal and physical, and most importantly, it feeds fear.

The Necessity of Death

Thirty-Nine deals with the concept of impending death. *Hometown Cha Cha Cha* does this as well, but the difference between them is age. In the first drama, the woman facing her mortality is young. Her death is shocking and somewhat cruel as she is finally developing into who she always needed to be. The second death in *Hometown Cha Cha Cha* is of a beloved and aging character. No less poignant and dreaded, this second character's impending death is met with a different emotional tone and repercussions. What both of these dramas do well is develop the emotional pull and soul-searching that precedes the passing of a loved one. A full range of reactions or denial is the heartstring of these pieces. Another drama that handles this topic particularly well is *Dear My Friends*. It addresses death and aging head-on in a way that is realistic, poignant, meaningful, and relatable.

The lesson here with these dramas is, if you are going to handle big topics, don't be afraid to dive deep. Fully explore the fallout, the emotion, the collateral damage to other characters. People react differently to loss and grief, and you'll be doing your readers a disservice if you don't honor those differences. Because isn't it true that when we read a book or watch a film we look for reflections of our own experiences, or the opposite, so that we can experience more in our own short revolution upon this earth?

Real World Problems

Real world problems are relatable to any audience, even in fantastical settings. If the situation is formatted so that the reader/ viewer can identify with the situation or feeling, then there is forged a natural connection, and with connection comes a relationship. Tragedies have real world counterparts, even in fantasy storylines, so that the audience (reader) can emotionally engage. These relationships are what we want to foster with our readers, especially if we want longevity in this business. Much of our sales is based on word-of-mouth, and frankly, with all that is going on in the world, in order to be part of the conversation, any conversation, our words must be memorable. "Real world" means our focus can't be something that only applies to the rich, elite, and only fantastical. Sure, we like reading Jane Austin and visiting the world of *Downton Abbey*, but if there were no common folk in either of those storylines, would we really tune in or read?

Smaller issues, while perhaps less dramatic, have more resonance if we can create an emotional connection or memory that helps us relate to the character. Not many of us will get a job overseas or marry a prince, but we can perhaps feel the pressure of that first meeting for a high status job review or trying to impress a future in-law. These are the moments that make our hearts race and are largely universal. Korean Drama writers know this and make us care for the main characters by these emotional touch-points as they navigate these waters.

Common fears could be a good way to make that initial connection with your reader/viewer. PTSD, specifically, claustrophobia is one explored in the drama, *Rain or Shine*. This drama is based on a building collapse. Through the shared background of this tragedy, several of the primary players in this drama deal with the literal emotional and financial fallout of being the surviving family member of a catastrophe. The word "survivor" even takes on many different meanings.

Whatever the dramatic reasoning for the claustrophobia, audience members can all relate to the feeling, even if we do not suffer the crippling fear. We have, at one time of another, been locked in a closet, been forgotten in a game of hide-and-go-seek, or had a basement door jam shut behind us, plunging us into momentary panic. Those few seconds for the majority of us is enough to at least evoke empathy with the characters in the drama. When we can empathize with a character, he or she is no longer just a name on a page or script, but a person. Then we can extend our shared history with the fear presented by the catastrophe and at least recall the nervous tension we felt. We are, therefore, utilizing our own memories and experiences to up the stakes.

Korean Drama is using the words between, the unwritten lines that exist because the reader or viewer personalizes and extends the reaction by making his or her own connections. It is as if in these dramas the events and characters are created in such a way that they spark a synapse of shared living, and in that leap, the magic happens. I would contend it is genius in its execution. How else could one explain the ever expanding draw of the medium that isn't even in our language? For American viewers, it takes work to view a Korean Drama: reading, rewinding the playback to re-read when the captioned text flows too quickly, and purposely evaluating physical cues the entire time we are viewing. However, the payoff is large and the investment in our efforts feels well-rewarded. That's good writing.

The results of this skilled world building and word play is connectivity. We can watch another person weather the issues on the screen while nursing our own fears and scars. All of this yields a greater awareness of audience for what is left unsaid. This is an important lesson in not overwriting. Give your readers some credit and allow them their role. For it is with the reader's connection that stories reach the soul (aka: stay in the memory and are quick off the tongue when someone asks for a recommendation). Proof of this is in your own memory. When you reflect back on books or films that stayed with you, it usually wasn't because of a sculpted line or page but how the piece made you feel or think.

An example of this empathic connection is in *This Is My First Life* (2017) where they presented the problem of families taking advantage of a daughter's role, especially as she is the new daughter-in-law. The implication is not only the status of being a new member of the family, but the need to impress the in-laws so that they would support the new union, and specifically, the new member. However, this quickly escalates into a passive-abusive relationship with the only winners the recipients of free labor. The awkward looks, the wringing of hands, the furtive glances and outright disapproval are developed in the drama, and not skimmed over as unimportant. Family drama is drama after all. And it is in this connection that the audience/reader can sympathize and start hoping for a resolution. Oftentimes, scenes such as these are merely touched on and then left, the point made. But here, the continued return to the issue helps to deepen the connection, reminds us of the agony, and internalize the suffering until we bring our own emotion into the piece. The actor no longer has to say a word, but rather, it is in his or her movements we interpret the weight of the familial pressure.

So, too, we need to write these nuances into our texts. Yes, he said this and then she said that, but what did these characters feel? Writers are often told to reduce or eliminate their adjectives. Then what should stand in their place? This. These small life moments need to be developed in a way that we can relate but with a light hand. As writers, we need to lead, not lecture. Readers do not need to be told what to think (although it is becoming a common convention to explain a scene as it unfolds in a film). Trust your reader to understand why this scene, this moment, matters. How can you assure this? Provide them with a dose of reality and a motive or stake that resonates. Both in fiction and fantasy, we must anchor our worlds in a way that is relatable to our reading audience or our words are nothing more than a story of little consequence.

Realism and Disability

Korean Drama is not afraid of dealing with exceptionalities, such as autism, as seen in *Extraordinary Attorney Woo* or *It's Okay Not to Be Okay* (2020) and does so without over sentimentality and romanticism. These characters are not a "token" representation but have a clear personality development and emotional span. In *Extraordinary Attorney Woo* (2022), the drama reveals the hopes, dreams, and fantastical ideas of Young-woo as the main character sees them in her head, from her waking obsession with whales to her problem-solving schematics. The writers also carefully plotted out and orchestrates the fantastical look of her thought processes and include physical movement idiosyncrasies, nervous ticks, and awkward gestures to round out her character development.

For an actor to portray physical and emotional ticks, eye avoidance, and mannerisms, they would have to either have shadowed someone (or several someones) for days to acquire ideas on how to "play" that character, or it is written into the script. For the sake of a book, what matters is how these characteristics are conveyed. We must think of our characters as a whole person, rather than a flat creation on a page. The audience needs to learn about their protagonists slowly and organically. All this fine attention to detail and nuance is what makes Attorney Woo endearing and draws further engagement. When dealing with a marginalized character, the writing needs to answer the question of what's at stake without being a caricature. Woo's lack of eye contact, echolalia, (she hears what is said repeated in her head), trips and triggers, do not represent a 2-D character but rather a fully, fleshed-out person that is handled with respect. She most definitely is not a mere novelty.

The writer considered how everyday things that we take for granted might be challenging for her. From her odd gate to her inability to process emotion, every action and reaction is considered. Her fixation with whales and avoidance of loud tones are childlike but not childish. The writer considered everything, including how others react in response. It is in the observance of all the components that make Attorney Woo who she is and gives her character credibility and humanity that we, the audience, can relate and connect to in a genuine way..

THIRTY-NINE (2022)

Writer: Yoo Young-A
Genre: Drama, romance
Produced by: Lotte Cultureworks & JTBC Studios

One theme in this K-drama is that while Death isn't fair, the bonds of true friendship last forever. In this realistic depiction, it becomes clear that there will be no last minute reprieve, no grand gesture to correct the course, and that simplicity is powerful. The second focus of this drama delves into the lives of three women and how they deal with the terminal illness of Chan-young. The story details the life of these friends and explores the minutia of their worries and daily tasks. The character of each woman is revealed by her life choices. While there is a romantic component to this storyline, the predominant love story is between the three friends.

This could be a good story for those who write cozy, not for the "happy ending" as that obviously won't happen in this story, but for all the little details that make for a rich storyline and yield an emotive response from the audience.

RAIN OR SHINE (2017)

Writer: Yoo Bo-ra
Genre: Drama (trauma and its aftermath)
Produced by: Celltrion Entertainment

Trauma is the buzzword for many current popular books and movies, but this drama shows the after effects and long-reaching impact of one such event. This is a prime example of "show, don't tell" that you hear so much about.

The primary male protagonist, Kang-doo, is scarred, literally, from the event that shapes his life, the collapse of a popular shopping mall, destroying his dreams of becoming a professional athlete. From that moment forward, and after years of physical therapy, his feelings of self-worth shape his goals and future path. The subsequent financial struggles and sacrifices he makes moving forward prove that he no longer feels he has his own life to lead. He is on a bitter trajectory, doing whatever he needs to in order to survive. But Kang-doo has no autonomy in his mind, no real choices as the future he imagined was wiped out with the collapse of the building. He is the caretaker of his sister, and in this new mindset, any risk is worth taking if it helps her.

The second male main character, Joo-won, loses his father in the same accident. The recursive blow destroys his father's reputation as lead architect, leaving a dark stain of shame and debt. This impacts Joo-won's career choices and his lingering lack of self-esteem. He possesses a strong work ethic partially imparted by a need to atone for the sins of the father, or so he is led to believe. The guilt he has assumed is encouraged by others and shapes his character and decision making.

The third main character, Moon-soo, links the trio. Unbeknownst to her, Kang-doo had been her savior during he mall collapse. She, too, bears the emotional scars of escaping death while her sister, and familial favorite daughter, did not. Both she and Kang-doo battle survivor's guilt and very real physical reactive stress to having been buried alive. Moon-soo is also the link to the young architect, Joo-won, who becomes her boss. The storylines and overlapping emotionality of one event is masterfully developed and portrayed in this multilayered storytelling.

CASTAWAY DIVA (2023)

Writers: Park Hye-ryun and Sun Yeol
Genre: Drama (trauma), coming of age, romance
Produced by: Studio Dragon and Baram Pictures

Soo Mok-ha is an idol-obsessed teen who hopes to audition and leave her small-town life and her father's oppressive control. Mok-ha shows her devotion to the diva, Ran-joo, learning her songs and studying her moves in hopes of living the life of a celebrity. But Ran-joo is hiding a secret, a botched vocal cord surgery. Her days as a singer are over, but she'd like to keep up the pretense— with help. A talent search is made for singers, similar in style to Ran-joo, making Mok-ha desperate for the opportunity to work with her hero. Aided by a self-sacrificing young man named Woo-hak, a young romantic interest, Mok-ha succeeds in escaping her father's eye to only get lost at sea and remains stranded for fifteen years.

Once rescued, Mok-ha resumes her dream of performing, although she is now a stranger to the modern world, having been excluded for so long. It's a story with a lot of heart and asks the question, when should you give up on a dream and when should you continue to believe?

Chapter Nine

NODS TO POP MEDIA

In K-drama, any nods to pop media are not superfluous. They can inspire suspense if the viewer knows the original social context, and it can keep a multi-age group interested. They are purposeful and useful as an analogy to convey content efficiently. For example, the *Rain Man* allusion in the opening credits of *It's Okay Not to Be Okay* gives context to the depth of the story through the quickly recognizable image of the two brothers walking at the start of the series. It is an easily recognizable reference that provides genre and tone in a few second glance. Even the tilt of the head and the costuming makes a direct reference to the film. Without dialogue or more than a few seconds of screen time, the viewer understands the context of the relationship. The writers took an easily recognizable image, based on the popularity of the film, that even if you didn't view the movie but only saw the promo materials, you could easily identify a core relationship between the brothers similar to the movie plot (an autistic older brother and the younger brother, bound by duty, loyalty, and love to support the elder.) In this way a connection is made. The viewer understands the emotional context and an unstated pact is made with the audience that this is what to expect.

Other examples include:

- *Cinderella and the Four Knights* tells us the main character's social status and her position within the family by just the title.

- The title, *Little Women*, tells us that, like the book of the same name, this drama will entail sisters, impoverished, with contrasting desires and motives, but tied together by familial love.

- In *Because This is My First Life*, the use and creation of a dating app, complete with the computer intel tells us not only time and place, but a bit about the socially awkward main character.

All of these serve as context anchors so that the reader (or viewer) engages quickly. In a world where numerous K-dramas exist, why should the person choose this one? Synonymous with the opening lines of the first chapter, the selection is a click away. There is only so much social-emotional real estate before the audience abandons one book for another. Worse yet, titles must hook the buyer in a minute or less.

The use of media creates social and cultural context. For example, a song lyric can reveal the inner emotion or inner voice of the character. It is not just a time stamp. Otherwise, your work could become dated, and subsequently, outdated quickly. So all music, lyric, band references are carefully thought out for more than social setting. Media references in K-drama serves as a hook to the financial or social context of the main characters. For example, the play, *Romeo and Juliet,* is still referenced in popular culture because we all understand and can identify with teen love, family feuds, and taking sides with friends. In K-drama, people compete for social promotion, fame, self-satisfaction and in yearning to break social ladder bonds.

A few examples of current tech and handling of social matters include:

- *Her Private Life* (2019) — topic: Fandom, the obsession with K-pop phenomenon
- *Celebrity* (2023) — topic: the dark side of social media and the need to be accepted and "liked" in a world of influencers and the depth of their power.
- *Doona* (2023) — topic: the pressures of being that celebrity and the pressure to perform and be perfect
- *Castaway Diva* (2023) topic: when fame fades and the social influence on an impressionistic teen.
- *My Halo Love* (2020) — topic: loneliness while surrounded by people, AI interactions, and technology

HER PRIVATE LIFE (2019)

Writer: Kim Hye-young
Genre: Romantic comedy, pop culture
Produced by: Studio Dragon and Bon Factory Worldwide

Sung Deok-mi leads a dual life in this timely Rom-com. She is an art curator at the prestigious Cheum Museum where her professionalism and diligence are unmatched. But in her private life she is a dedicated fan girl of the K-pop band, White Ocean, and specifically, lead singer Cha Si-an. A true super fan, she runs the fan site, "The Road to Si-an", even garnering the attention of the singer himself. Fan-girling costs Deok-mi not only money but sacrificed hours in chasing a chance sighting of the pop star as well as opportunity for true romance. Her obsession goes as far as making her home a shrine to Si-an.

Not long after the start of this drama, her museum has a change in leadership in the form of Ryan Gold, a Korean who spent much of his life abroad as a successful art critic. Ryan is known for his impeccable taste, his word inspiring investments or despair. His own art talents as a painter have dried up, so he turns his keen eye to bitter critiques.

When challenged by her new director, Deok-mi must reassess her fantasy man for a real life but no less elusive love interest. While normally she doesn't date, she must create the farce of dating Ryan to get Si-an's maniacal fans off her back.

CELEBRITY (2023)

Writer: Kim Yi-young
Genre: Thriller / Drama
Produced by: Studio Dragon

Celebrity focuses on the lives and challenges of media influencers. Through the pressure placed on the main protagonist, we learn of the destructive nature of the drive for wealth, power, and followers. Shown through the behavior of a collective of assertive and ethically bankrupt influencers, *Celebrity* highlights the drive for elevated social standing in a fickle and ever-evolving media world. The drama explores the underbelly of media influencers and their thirst for power, money, and prestige as well as the games played to move ahead. The drama highlights the lengths these women will go to acquire status and how they destroy others without pangs of conscience.

The storytelling format is developed though flashback, from beyond the grave of one victim, who uniquely reveals the volatile and destructive nature of influencers and their breaking points between the rise and fall of their social status. The fact that the story is shown in what appears to be present tense and then evolves into something more makes this K-drama both thrilling and confusing. The writers skillfully crafted the unraveling of the story to intrigue and evade an easy resolution, making the viewer eager for the next installment of the story. Likewise, the cast of characters are not all that they seem upon first meeting, and they, too evolve as the story develops.

MY HALO LOVE (2020)

Writers: Ryu Yong-jae, Kim Han-chae, Choi Sung-joon
Genre: Science Fiction, romance, drama
Produced by: Studio Dragon

My Halo Love explores the theme of loneliness, belonging, and the need for connection in this awkward romance involving a hologram and a timid eyewear employee. This romance could've easily turning into a light-hearted comedic romp as previous AI/human interactions have been portrayed; however, these writers addressed the very real issues of doubt, insecurity, isolation, and the difficulties our modern world creates in forming meaningful relationships. Likewise, the AI love interest has a very real, human counterpart and creator who struggles with intimacy in favor of being hidden in the computer world. This gets further complicated as he develops feelings for her. *My Halo Love* answers the anticipated questions about a relationship with a hologram without pandering and while staying true to the point of view of the main characters. The real life issues are nuanced and detailed in such a believable way that the viewer is engaged by the logic and immersive structure of this tale.

The female protagonist, So-yeon, of this tale is face-blind, unable to recognize even her co-workers. Her hologram, nested in her advanced AI specs, helps her see in a way that had been denied to her in the years following a traumatic event. However, the tech proves to be a security risk for darker schemes. While integral to develop an emotional attachment with another, the two-sided romance seems doomed from the start, but the deft skills of these writers successfully keep emotion the true focus.

Embedded triggers in the sensory details, flashes of memory, and visual cues reveal So-yeon's true character. The strength of this K-drama lies in the fact that every portion of the fantastical and scientific elements are researched and believable, making this tale both plausible and viable to our modern reality.

Chapter Ten

BEGINNINGS AND ENDINGS

The Initial Hook

People often think the hook is how you start a book. It is, and it isn't. You can initially create it as you start writing, but like this little book, I suggest you revisit this closer to the end. The hook is a promise to the the reader of tone, mood, and focus. If you haven't written your book yet, can you be sure that what you promised is what will be fulfilled? I don't care if you are a meticulous planner, Revisit your hook. Something might have changed or you may have learned something about your characters and their troubles that gives you better clarity. I can promise you this, in a K-drama, those first few minutes in the opening scene set the tone, and the ensuing drama stays true to its promise.

In the hook, the main character reveals much of his or her own character. It starts with point of view. From the onset we know if this will be his or her story. Within moments we know something he or she values, the stakes, and their level of stress or urgency. Audience is immediately immersed. Viewers or readers are increasingly impatient. They read or watch for but moments before making a judgement. What K-drama does is optimize those first few moments. Readers or viewers want to be grabbed, so entice them. The problem is that audiences do not connect with characters they do not empathize with. So how do we handle this?

Toss your characters into the story midstream. How do they react? What choices do they make? Better yet, reveal their thought processes by a hesitation, a nervous hand gesture, panicked and darting eyes. Make me, the reader, want to know more. K-drama's strength is in these opening moments. Within five minutes there has been character development, something immediately at stake, nuanced character movement or ticks, and the first of many obstacles has appeared, predictable or not. Even caste or class has been indicated (grubby sneakers, unemployed and making kimchi, being lost and looking for an address with panic on his or her face, or straightening a designer tie or handbag).

So what does the reader need to know now? It certainly is not a full character description. Clothes change as do situations, but mannerisms, stressors, thinking or reasoning patterns, and movement do not. Make your character "act fast" to a situation and see what happens.

The Initial Hook

It is true, no one will read your words if you haven't first hooked them. But if you lie to them in the hook, they will never read your words again. K-drama even goes one step further, using opening animation (including sometimes internal illustration), and teaser clips to provide a snapshot of what's to come and to lure the audience into giving their drama a chance. There are many examples of this, but the following can give you a quick idea of what is possible: *Doom at Your Service, Little Women,* and *It's Okay Not to Be Okay*.

So what does this this have to do with you, the novelist? In those opening lines, create a scene rich with imagery and character development so that the reader can identify the main character and the problem, at least the most immediate one, and make us care.

The opening pages were stress-inducing for me. I'd rewrite, rewrite, and rewrite in hopes of making the action pop without feeling rushed. The pressure to present a character in the first few minutes was overwhelming. How could I possibly give the reader an accurate representation of my main character without "telling" and likewise, how do I reflect her personality with spoilers? It seems impossible.

It was the opening of a K-drama that was the proverbial light through the fog for me. Take some time and just watch the first fifteen minutes of a drama and make a list of what the writers have shown you: character, problem (at least the immediate one), and emotion. Then if you can tear yourself away, try another drama. The more I watched, the easier it became to envisage my own opening lines. Give it a try. You've nothing to lose and everything to gain.

Cover Design

Another form of hook, and a powerful one, is in the cover design. In just a handful of seconds the intro graphics in a K-drama indicate the tone, genre, and reveal a few key plot points. You need to do the same with your cover. While you may not initially understand all the illustrations at the start of your drama, by the end of the series, all has been revealed. All along, the art had been truthful in its promise of what was to come, although sometimes teasingly or coy. You, as a writer, have the same thirty seconds with your cover (much like an elevator pitch). Your cover can be innovative, alluring and elusive but also true to the content or you'll betray your readers' trust.

I, personally, love to watch the intro graphics over several episodes of the series, as the more I know of the evolving storyline, the richer the art becomes. Oftentimes, the graphics shift as the story unravels, creating interesting tidbits of new data (character development and plot) to mull over. You can choose to do this with interior details at chapter headings, chapter art, or even a teasing quote. Likewise, I enjoy a cover that provides an image that becomes almost a symbol as to what I should feel or take away. The cover or thumbnail, is essentially the literary amuse-bouche of the juicy storyline.

On an important note, test your cover as a thumbnail. As people scroll the internet, will your cover catch their eye or yield interest? All that fine detail in some truly beautiful artwork will be lost when sunk into less than an inch. Think color, pop, and key imagery to bait the hook.

One thing to consider, too, is the quality of your cover. Saving a few bucks now may cost you in the long run. When you think about the beautiful animation and page design for K-dramas, it is clear that they spared no expense because they know that the eye is the initial draw. If the cover sparks an interest, or in the drama's case, makes you tune in when there are so many other offerings available, the cost is justified.

Questions to ask yourself are:

-How will your book attract on a bookshelf or in a thumbnail?

- Is your cover vibrant and enticing?

- Is it true to the tone and theme of your story?

- Does it give a clear indicator of the type or genre or story you will portray?

- Is the text legible? Is there good contrast in colors to help with that?

- Does the imagery you have chosen really reflect the content of your book in some way?

Titles

Perhaps the first place people overlook is their title. Your title MUST have impact immediately. With the glut of dramas gracing the screen, how did they lure you into stopping to watch theirs? With novels, you would have to multiply that variable to an incalculable number to reach the sheer number of books there are in the world. Help your reader find you by your title.

One thing to note, your title cannot be copyrighted. That being said, I do not advise your abscond with someone else's title. That is a good way to confuse your reader and annoy the writer or the earlier work. While there is a vast number of titles to choose from in the world, the internet makes that world a small place. Yes, it will be noticed. Yes, it can be a bid deal. Can your title be totally original? Not always. I would just be wary that your chosen title hasn't been used in the recent past and that your category for your piece is dramatically different. Take the time to find the book's true name.

Titles should:

- Intrigue and entice
- Be fun (if appropriate for genre)
- Be definitive of tone and genre
- Can possibly be a pun
- Have an occasionally literary spin such as *Little Women* or *Cinderella and the Four Knights*

Should not:

- Be misleading in tone or content
- Be so "cute" that they are distracting to the main storyline

For my own personal preference, I tend to choose two to three word titles (this book being the exception). For novels, the mood and genre is what is most important to convey. If you are writing a series, it is best to be consistent with the titles as well. If your first two books have a three word title, so should the subsequent books. Independent books can be individualized. Think, too, about font and printing. A shorter title means your title can be larger and perhaps easier to recognize on a sales hosting sire. For a final test, ask your Beta reads if the title matches their impression of the book.

A Satisfying Resolution

A satisfying resolution should not be confused with a happy ending and especially not a "miracle" ending. The resolution should not be a "given". While there is some formula to Korean Drama, nothing is promised other than in those labeled as romance. The main character will end up happy in that genre, but not necessarily with the person or in the situation you anticipated. If the ending were neatly wrapped up as a convention, that would be cheating the reader / viewer of the delicious tension of the unknown. How can they feel for a character when there are no stakes, no risk? You are also betraying the faith the readers put in you so many pages ago. They want a story to transport them, to thrill, and create an emotion in them. Do not short-change your readers. If you go straight from point A to point B without any tension, any unknowns, a lack of surprise and suspense, your reader will quickly lose faith in your ability to sculpt a believable tale, and even worse, they may never trust you again when you put out new work.

A reader might initially give you the benefit of the doubt. If things in the story seem to progress too easily but they keep reading, they are waiting for the trick, the twist, the turn where their emotional and time investment will pay off. Simply put, they read because they have faith in your ingenuity. The purchase of your book is a contract of sorts. They literally bought into the belief that you have a story to tell. You, the writer, have to fulfill the promise. And it shouldn't be the same story they've seen or read before. Give them something new and engaging. And where some studios have a style to their dramas, in my experience, they all pride themselves in their unique storytelling.

Everyone doesn't nor shouldn't get a happy ending. Oftentimes good people die, and sometimes far too young. Some remain broken-hearted, while others never seem to be able to learn a lesson. Such is life. And the best art imitates life. Shouldn't this apply, too, to our stories? K-drama excels in this concept.

Like real life, all storylines should not wrap up at the same time. Sure, we talk about having babies at the same time as our friends or going into business together, but lives do not align like that, nor should your book. Some characters have more growth needed; some are just beginning, and others are still hopelessly lost. There were several characters that had tragic endings in *The Uncanny Counter*. The good were not always saved nor deserved their fates. Similarly, those most deserving of retribution don't always get it. Sometimes the bad guy gets away. That realism, and frustration, feeds the reader/viewer. Anytime an audience sees life resonating in their fantasy, as in *The Uncanny Counter*, the reader knows that the writer has invested credibility into the writing. They may not like the end result for a few characters, but the time spent in crafting a believable outcome, even in fantastical genres, pays off on the storytelling. Likewise, knowing that each character's life won't tie up neatly, creates an anxious engagement that keeps us on the edge of our seats.

In *Our Beloved Summer* (2021) when Ung and Yeon-soo revisit their emotional past after many years, each key character has evolved and grown. However, the summer memories and feelings prove complicated and confused. The non-linear timeline and unpredictable outcome keeps the viewer eagerly tuning in for more.

The Back Blurb

Simply put, the back blurb should focus on a character development and setting, plotting continual social and emotional stakes. It is the shortest thing you will write and possibly the most important.

Take the time to really work on the blurb. It sometimes can feel like writing a summary of your novel without revealing too much is an impossible task. It truly is a tough task, especially since you are so close to your work. Maybe have a Beta reader help you with defining it. Identify the stakes for your character and start there. You could review some of the write up for K-dramas on whatever video hosting site you use. Better yet, read the write ups of the dramas you have already watched. What key elements did they include? Where did they leave it vague and yet inviting?

The extra effort you take in crafting your back blurb will pay off. I promise. Remember, your reader, if they get past the front cover and want to know more, will next flip the book to the back cover and read. Did you give them enough info that they know what type of book it is? Is there a character and a problem identified? If it then makes them open the front cover, you have won the battle.

You could also go to the first five minutes of any K-drama. What did they promise in those first few minutes? That's what you should include on your blurb.

My final advice is do not let someone else write it for you. They can make suggestions or offer a template, but ultimately you need to identify your work clearly and concisely. And for goodness sakes, do not let AI do it for you. The last thing you need is AI generic drivel.

The Last Character

The last character is the audience, and the Korean drama industry clearly identified and understands who they are writing for. I've always read and heard that you should write with your audience in mind. Clearly K-drama does as they garner new and wider audiences daily. I, personally, write the stories I want to read and then think of who to market them for- and maybe that is flawed. So what is the right conclusion? However you decide to write your work, once you have vented your story, in whatever format feels correct to the storyline, step back and think about what K-drama does well, and how can you edit and sharpen your own words to make the impact that these dramas do. If anything, think about the promise a new book makes to its audience and start to fulfill that on page one through five, just as the dramas do in those precious first moments on the screen. Writers of all formats, are hoping to share our vision with others, so it's time to factor your reader into the formula.

THANK YOU

Thank you for reading my thoughts on my addiction to K-drama and the many things I have learned from their talented writers. It is my hope that you tune in and discover series that touch your heart and perhaps refine your pen.

Please pass along to me your new K-drama discoveries. I can be reached at:

rebeccawynick.com
rebeccawynick@gmail.com
Facebook @ Rebecca Wynick

If you enjoyed this book, please consider posting a review, even a star without a comment helps this book gain visibility.

LIST OF REFERENCED K-DRAMAS

(Featured noted with an asterisk*)

Because This Is My First Life (2017)*
Business Proposal (2022)
Castaway Diva (2023)*
Celebrity (2023)*
Cinderella and the Four Knights (2016)*
Crash Landing on You (2020)*
Dear My Friends (2016)*
Do Do Sol Sol La La Sol (2020)
Doom, at Your Service (2021)
Doona (2023)
Extraordinary Attorney Woo (2022)*
Heavenly Ever After (2025)*
Her Private Life (2019)*
Hometown Cha -Cha-Cha (2021)*
Hotel Del Luna (2019)*
It's Okay Not to Be Okay (2020)*
Little Women (2022)*
Love Next Door (2024)
Miss Day and Night (2024)

My Demon (2023)
My Halo Love (2020)*
My Liberation Notes (2021)*
My Unfamiliar Family (2020)*
Nevertheless (2021)*
Our Beloved Summer (2021)*
Our Unwritten Seoul (2025)*
Potato Lab (2025)*
Rain or Shine (2017)*
Romance Is a Bonus Book (2019)*
Run On (2020)
Start Up (2020)*
Thirty - Nine (2022)*
The Uncanny Counter (2020)*

Just watch. If at the end of the first episode and you don't care, move on. Most will not disappoint. Sometimes it simply is you were not in the mood for that particular subject matter

ACKNOWLEDGMENTS

No book can be born without the help of people surrounding the author. In this case my family was key to getting this book done.

Watching and rewatching K-dramas was patiently tolerated, as were the late night maddening editing sessions. (The lapses in proper grammar were actually choices... I wanted the book to be more conversational than academic and therefore, further removed from the reader.)

However, I struggled with the direction to take with this book. I started and stopped, rewrote and trashed with equal measure until finally landing on a more conversational and hopefully, accessible book.

Paige Christie completed the final formatting of the cover and tech processing of the final text so that this little book could be produced.

But my champion was my husband, Jerry, who cooked or got take-away so that I could find the time to write and create. He sacrificed his weekends and evenings to make my world just a little bit softer (with so many tasks) so that I could do what drives me. You have my heart and a huge debt of gratitude. Thanks, honey — you're the best. I'm a very lucky girl.

ABOUT THE AUTHOR

Born Rebecca Sánchez, Wynick often reflects on the people and places of her youth, relocating some of her favorite haunts into her fictional settings. Missing her beloved Catskill Mountains, she moved to the foothills of western North Carolina. While Asheville is a place of wondrous beauty, she still misses New York diners, pizza, and Kosher delis (to name a few).

Wynick spends her days largely in the past, teaching about dead, British writers. On weekends, she enjoys treasure hunting with her husband, collecting antique typewriters, blown glass, and pottery from local artists. Her grown children inspire her to keep following her passion for writing, and she occasionally thanks them with homemade cheesecake. Her cat is not so easily impressed.

Wynick hopes that you reach out and say hello if you enjoyed her book. She'd love to hear from you. Check out her website @rebeccawynick.com or other social media.

 bsky.app/profile/rebeccawynick.bsky.social

 facebook.com/rebecca_wynick

 instagram.com/rebecca_wynick

ALSO BY REBECCA WYNICK

Novels:

Amber Witch

Dolmen Echo (coming soon)

Short Story Collection:

Twists of Fate

Anthology contributor:

Witches, Warriors, and Wise Women

Become Legend, 2021 JordanCon Anthology

The Leaf Does No Harm, 2023 JordanCon Anthology

www.ingramcontent.com/pod-product-compliance
Lightning Source LLC
LaVergne TN
LVHW051004080826
845145LV00009B/2453

* 9 7 8 1 9 5 3 0 7 4 2 1 8 *